GW00457728

Practical Spirituality – A Guide

Twelve tools to raise the vibration of your consciousness, find your purpose and embrace your spiritual aspirations—without living in a cave

First published in UK 2023
by Anthony Oyo

ISBN: 9798398570977

Cover art by Kathryn Burrington
www.mandalameadow.com

Consciousness Awaken

For Eliza and Max

CONTENTS

Twelve stories

Acknowledgements

MY DEEPLY felt gratitude goes out to those many beautiful spirits and souls, those with us now and those in other realms, who supported the creation of this book. Especially Christina, David, Estelle, Isabella, Jan, Nigel, Sharon, Sheila, Sue, Suzanne and Elijah Otim for saying yes and for their courage in creating their stories to share with others seeking to draw inspiration from their own challenges and successes. And for those who were genuine in their desire to contribute, and found the alignment not quite right, yet … many thanks, and there is always the sequel!

My sincere appreciation to Kathryn for guidance and patience through the mandala design journey and David for helping to ground my prose back to Planet Earth and guiding me through the process of getting this out to you, the reader. To Sue and Nige, for your challenge. It was uncomfortable … but gratefully received.

To all the questioning and wisdom of our ancestors and contemporaries that have aided and inspired the creation of this book, my eternal thanks.

And thanks to so many others who patiently listened to the story of 'The Book' over the years. Well here it is, I can shut up now. Until the next one. Namaste.

Introduction

WHY ARE you reading this introduction … and why should you continue?

Everything is as it should be, right here and right now. This may not always be easy to believe, but it's probably the case that if you are reading this introduction, you are searching. Perhaps you've been searching for some time, and the questions that you've been asking include some of the following:

- Why do I feel lost?
- Why do I feel stuck, or at a crossroads in my life/career?
- Why do I feel out of balance with the world?
- I know intuitively that my spiritual interests should play a more substantial part in my life, but how do I combine them with my everyday routines and responsibilities?
- What is my life purpose?
- How can I meditate regularly?
- Why are most people around me not interested in discussing spirituality?
- How can I attend more retreats?
- How might I combine my spiritual interest with achieving progression in my job?
- How can I balance my spirituality with my home responsibilities?

- How do I handle being the only spiritual person in my family?
- How can I achieve abundance?

At some point in our lives, many of us become aware of something 'higher' or 'elsewhere' or 'up there' or ... (fill in the blank). Apparently, it can't be seen or touched, but it's important, affects everything, has been around forever, knows everything and sometimes even 'knows if we've been bad or good'. Not everyone believes it exists, but most people do, and have done across all the ages of human existence.

This book was written to help you achieve practical spirituality in your life: that is, to work through the challenges and practicalities of leading your spiritual life and journey, recognising the very real obstacles that everyday life appears to throw in your path to achieving that. This includes the pressures imposed by work, family and finances, societal and global issues, as well our own doubts in ourselves. This last point is important: all too often we are unsure of our abilities and visions and adopt limiting self-beliefs, that appear emboldened by their success in preventing our growth, expansion and taking risks.

The approach of this book is in part influenced by the ancient techniques of using storytelling to teach and present information, which continues today very successfully. The approach adopts the idea of using the power of narrative to overcome challenges, real or apparent, in order to give us the skills and courage to live a spiritual life.

Not surprisingly, this book draws heavily on my own life and the story of my own spiritual journey, as well as stories from other sources that have inspired me. I have been fortunate to collect eleven of these from my fellow travellers, some of them family, friends and colleagues, who have taken the time to articulate how practical spirituality has presented itself in their daily lives. These tales from other extraordinary humans (I don't think anyone is 'ordinary') share the vast knowledge and rich experiences that exist among us. I am deeply grateful for their contributions and know that you, the reader, will resonate with some, if not all, of their journeys.

In what follows, I give twelve practical steps for the reader to consider, and twelve personal stories that go some way to illustrate them. That figure is not arbitrary. I believe the number twelve to be important and powerful in our reality, and one that gives us the potential to tap into unseen forces, on many levels, that can empower and increase the range and impact of actions, ideas and intentions. The front cover illustration of a twelve-sided Mandala design was specifically commissioned for this book, and wonderfully created by UK-based artist Kathryn Burrington (www.mandalameadow.com). The number twelve talks to us from our ancient past, and is present in our everyday life. Consider the following:

- Twelve is present on the clock face, where it divides the Earth's revolutions on its axis. It is present on the calendar, where is does the same work for the Earth's revolution around the sun.
- In human biology, the body has twelve systems, and some believe the number of key chakras to be twelve.
- The Waoroni tribe in Ecuador, who made their first contact with the rest of humanity only in the 1950s, have a significant prevalence of babies born with six fingers and toes, and this condition (polydactyly) is not uncommon. Ancient cave art throughout the world depicts humanoids and other creatures with six fingers and toes, for example those found in Chaco

Canyon in New Mexico and Newspaper Rock in Utah.

- In the Old Testament, there are twelve tribes of Israel; in the New Testament, Jesus had twelve apostles; in Greek mythology, twelve titans fought twelve Olympians; in Celtic myths there were twelve knights seated at Arthur's Round Table.
- Neolithic stone circles often have twelve megaliths in their outer rings. This is the case at Gobekli Tepe in Turkey, built at least 11,500 years before the present (BP); the Stones of Stenness in the Orkney (circa 5,100 BP), the Callanish Stones in the Outer Hebrides (circa 5,000 BP).
- The Mayan calendar was based on factors of twelve and the Sumerian cuneiform number system was sexagesimal—that is, it used a base of sixty, of which twelve is a factor.
- Pythagoras (2,500 BP) worked out that music is divided into twelve notes. An octave has twelve steps to it, and that is the basis of the mathematics of music.
- In July 2012, the Large Hadron Collider at CERN, near Geneva, detected the existence of the Higgs boson, the so-called God particle. This is the twelfth fundamental particle, and the detection completed the Standard Model of particle physics (that is, the theory that describes all the known fundamental particles, how they interact and—with the Higgs—why some of them have mass).

Thirty years after my 'conscious awakening', and drawing on a diverse global Corporate Engineering background, and now as a qualified Spiritual Life Coach and Reiki Master Healer and Teacher, I am ready to share the methods and strategies that I have considered and tried in order to redefine and achieve my dreams and aspirations, and how I balanced my life and spiritual goals with the realities, challenges and practicalities of everyday life. This has helped me to acquire and develop an understanding of what the human experience actually is and the incredible benefits that come from reconsidering human 'be-ing' from an alternative paradigm.

Through my journey, I've recognised the spiritual support needs of people who've decided not to escape the norms of society by going off to live an alternative lifestyle. This is not a judgment, it's simply a recognition that for many people, the decision to continue to be engaged with the responsibilities that come with jobs, careers, mortgages, material aspirations, families and the trappings of a more conventional lifestyle is a conscious one. But at the same time, they still have the desire to progress their spiritual journeys. I do not believe the two are mutually exclusive, and this book has been written with the specific purpose of helping and guiding people to find a balance whereby they can achieve their aspirations in their spiritual and everyday lives.

My own story, which led to the creation of this book, started before I was born. It began in the ether, when and where the idea of my unique experience was first conceived. In terms of my conscious awakening, that happened when I was twenty-two years old. This is explained in more detail—along with the other eleven fantastic stories—after each of the twelve steps, but here it is in brief.

My conscious awakening began when I graduated with an engineering degree and started my graduate training in a heavily industrialised city in the central UK. My corporate life was off to a good start: I had a good job, a decent salary and opportunities to build a career. I rented a cheap, rather grubby studio flat in the red-light area. My neighbour, Ed Sherwood, was a crop circle savant with an extremely different background to mine. He later went on to become a significant presence in the world of crop circle research and founded Millennium Research, along with his future wife Kris. At the time of our meeting, we were young men living in our bedsits and exploring life through young eyes. Although we were very different people, for instance he had a close working relationship with the mice in his bedsit and I certainly did not with mine, we became friends and engaged in some amazing meaning-of-life conversations.

Through these conversations with Ed I was introduced to the idea that all is not as it seems, that life and existence are far more complex than they appear, and that we are not alone in the universe. This was 1991 and although it had been a few years since the release of movies such as *Close Encounters of the Third Kind* and *ET the Extra-Terrestrial* and despite the huge success of the first three *Star Wars* movies, the idea of ET being real and here on Earth was generally considered pretty crazy. He lent me a copy of *The Only Planet of Choice: Essential Briefings from Deep Space*, (Schlemmer & Jenkins, 1993). These are a series of channelled messages, received over a period of twenty years from non-Earthly cosmic beings called the Council of Nine. They were compiled by Phyllis V Schlemmer (a deep-trance medium) and the polymath Palden Jenkins. The group receiving these communications included some well-known people, such as the racing driver Sir John Whitmore, Olympic runner David Hemery, scientist Andrija Puharich, psychic performer Uri Geller, *Star Trek* originator Gene Roddenberry and others such as biologist Lyall Watson and Werner Erhard, the founder of Erhard Seminars Training (EST).

At this time, I was not aware or interested in the scepticism surrounding channelling. I loved *Star Trek*. I loved the idea that the concept of the 'prime directive' had, so it was said, come from Roddenberry's engagement with the Council of Nine. And, at a deeper level, the idea that the Earth has a history quite different to conventional understanding just made sense to me.

So, life progressed. I explored this alternative aspect of existence in parallel with my corporate life. My first engineering job after my graduate training was in Southampton, and I continued my spiritual growth there, exploring meditation and all things 'other'. This was before the coming of the internet or Amazon, so it was the beginning of my perusals of mind, body and spirit bookshops—a pastime that I've since carried on across the globe over thirty years. I still have books from where it all began, the Stellar Gateway bookshop in Carlton Place, Southampton, which is sadly no longer there.

My professional career progressed well. I climbed the corporate ladder and gained leadership roles at a young age. A diversion into international development took me into the world of government, the World Bank Group and multilateral agencies; I lived in Washington, DC, and I travelled all over the world. At the same time, I was developing my meditation practice, experiencing the natural energies of structures such as Stonehenge and Avebury, exploring Buddhism and challenging my teachers in that discipline with my need for ever more detail. Within a few years, my personal world and responsibility grew from just one (me), to two and then the joys and challenges of small family life.

At this point, the need to support my new family became my dominant life focus, and my spiritual journey took a break for quite a few years. However, my intuitive 'knowing' that there was more to life remained constant, even if I wasn't able to pay it the attention I would have liked to. Over the following years I branched out into consulting, I created my own renewable energy business and I was approached to lead an investment project in New Zealand. I spent six years there, and this is where my spiritual calling kicked back in with my introduction to reiki energy healing.

Time and my life had progressed for these two parallel selves until, after about twenty years, there occurred what I can only describe as an external, otherworldly intervention: forces outside my control 'directed' the idea towards me that my dual lives must take a different path—or at least, that I needed to reflect consciously on the fact that there were two, and decide how I wanted them to develop … and take action. That moment, ten years ago, was pivotal to my becoming a reiki master healer and teacher. It was what led me to understand my life purpose and prepare myself to give back as a teacher, healer and life coach.

So now, in my early fifties, after a series of challenging and painful course corrections, I can say that I finally understand my life so far … the themes and the lessons and importance of the decisions that I created to make, and their consequences. I understand how I'm at the centre of my own creation, and I know my purpose: to raise the vibration of human consciousness. And the book you are reading now is a significant part of that purpose.

Activities such as writing, speaking, teaching, reiki energy healing, spiritual life coaching, running retreats and trying to live an aligned life are all part of the same theme, that of helping and encouraging others to raise their own, and thus the human collective's, vibrational energy. This is done in order to assist humanity to evolve into a more compassionate species and ultimately to take our place, with others, in the cosmos.

I see the first fifty years as my first two phases in this life: the preparation and prelude to my third and final phase. This is where I get to give back. This does not mean that this phase will be any easier than the previous two, but having this purpose, rather than searching for it, means that I can focus my activities and decisions on what aligns with my purpose, and can be aware, with the support of my spiritual practice, of those that do not. I feel blessed to be able to have awareness of the duality of my existence. I can be present inside 'the matrix' and can observe my responses and reactions from outside, too.

In working with the other authors who've lovingly and courageously shared their stories in this book, I created eight questions for them to consider, the first being 'how would you describe your spirituality?' You will see that each response was different. For me … I know I am an incarnation on Earth, in this three-dimensional existence, of my higher self, my soul and spirit, and I am aware of the opportunities for growth that come through that knowledge and this experience. I know that my natural state is spirit. Therefore, my spirituality describes how I connect with my true self in order to be consciously connected and aware of all that is and to receive guidance from it and retain alignment with my true self and purpose.

The final question to the authors was 'What have you learned about your practical spirituality, and the human experience?' Again, the response differed across the authors. My lessons include:

- Life is not, by design, easy—but it is full of wonder.
- By raising your awareness, you raise your vibration, and you make the connection with, and awareness of, the universal energy of 'all that is' much easier. Entering meditative states

is key to this.

- The circumstances of your birth and childhood were designed to set your personal point of reference, from which you base your growth opportunities for the rest of your life. There are no coincidences.
- Practical spirituality, for most of us, is challenging. It requires a degree of selflessness and self-compassion, especially in a family structure. But other people's lack of understanding of your spiritual needs, the nature of your journey and your possible difficulties in articulating matters of 'faith' are not reasons not to pursue that which you need to.
- It's important to take action—and risks.

Through my journey I have been inspired and influenced by much wisdom, events and people—perhaps too much and too many to acknowledge everything and everyone here. However, I would like to mention in particular Tony Robbins (rmtcenter.com), Jack Canfield (www.jackcanfield.com), Dr Michael Beckwith (michaelbeckwith.com), and a number of the collaborators in Mind Valley (www.mindvalley.com).

2: Humanity: how are we doing?

BEFORE WE explore the meaning of the 'human experience', which we will do in the next chapter, let us take stock of where we are today.

As we approach the end of the first quarter of the twenty-first century, technology development is racing ahead at a great rate of knots, we all have access to much more information and many more possibilities than we have ever had before. A career aspiration to be an astronaut and interstellar explorer is now a reality for today's teenagers … And yet, something does not feel quite right.

Despite our technological feats, children under the age of five still die because their basic needs are not met, such as clean drinking water and access to basic health care. Extreme poverty, violent conflict, economic imbalance and injustice remain the calling card of Planet Earth. The global pandemic of 2020/21 brought into sharp relief the inequalities and dire consequences associated with poverty and their link to race and economic opportunity, or the lack of it. The pandemic also exposed the fragility of our systems of government and global management, often as a result of ego and arrogance, ignorance and group incompetence. And in many places around the world, it highlighted the consequences of populations' delegation of their responsibilities as democratic citizens, the failure to effectively manage our democratic processes and the frailties of the officials we voted into positions of responsibility on our behalf, often without any real check on their competence, or understanding of their personal motivations.

So, across the world today we are experiencing male energy, singular and insecure, driven by results and lacking in compassion. It is this energy that is defining the vibration of Planet Earth. Climate change can no longer be doubted: extreme weather events affect the whole planet on a regular basis. Although we all have access to unfathomable volumes of information, our privacy is threatened by small groups of faceless individuals and agencies busying themselves with the data generated by our existence. And across the planet, even before the Covid-19 lockdowns, instances of mental health challenges were increasing, with higher levels of depression and anxiety. Are we, therefore, plodding along at a normal evolutionary rate for a planet like ours, approaching 200 years of rapid technological growth and advancement, or is there more to this story? Are we actually experiencing some strange Groundhog Day nightmare in which, despite the outward appearance of minor change, the paradigm is endlessly repeated in new guises? That is, the have-nots keep not having, and maybe have less, whereas the haves keep on having, with a small number owning a greater share of the total pool of what there is to have. Maybe we are approaching a tipping point, where after thousands of years of spiritual confusion and an ever-growing disconnection from our environment, each other and our own selves, we reach a planetary crisis in which humanity's very existence is in doubt. And perhaps that will lead to a period of fundamental awakening, in which we all get to find out 'what it's all about' … why we are here, and what we are supposed to do with it!

This change will not happen on its own. It requires a paradigm shift from Earth's most conscious entities—homo sapiens. No one is coming to save us, we humans, who have messed up the planet and affected the energy flows of the universe. Mother Earth, or Gaia, will probably look after things if she needs to and that would mean ridding herself of the factor that is causing all the damage … that's right—us. Floods, earthquakes, tsunamis are all ready to hand in her Armageddon toolkit. There are some who believe this has happened before, perhaps many times before, for example the Biblical Flood of Noah, et al. There's no reason for it not to happen again, but wouldn't it be better for humanity to sort out our mess before we repeat the cycle? To grow up, finally, and elevate ourselves to the higher echelon of planetary custodians … showing that we can let go of selfish needs and ego, see the bigger picture, go beyond just talking about compassion and actually taking action and doing the right thing, at the right time, because it is the right thing to do—with all the sacrifices that it might entail …?

How can we achieve such a paradigm shift on an individual level? For many, this idea has been front and centre for their entire lives. An increasing number of others have become aware of it more recently. Perhaps constantly pinging their minds for years has been the idea of something else, something bigger, a greater purpose and the possibility of a greater connection with everything. Or maybe they found less and less meaning in the conventional story of who we are as a species, how we got here, our history and what we are here for … Perhaps it appeared too full of contradictions—a bunch of made-up stuff, clearly written to justify the actions of some man somewhere and somewhen.

So, we have the opportunity for a paradigm shift on a personal level. It is possible that only through such a shift will the epochal, planet-wide change that is our destiny happen. Many of us have felt the call of something else, a deep-rooted drive to reconnect with something 'other', more profound than our personal existence. It is this reconnection and realignment that will support our personal growth and the positive evolution of Planet Earth into its next phase. Perhaps we have reached that point, common to billions of planets in the cosmos, when the inhabitants finally get to grow up and realise they are not alone in the universe, that they are connected energetically to everything, and that there is a point and purpose to existence. Let's hope so!

3: The human experience

THIS CHAPTER proposes a response to the age-old question, 'why are we here?' and suggests what that answer means for living a practical, spiritually rewarding life. The idea presented here is not new. It can be found in many texts and explanations of the human experience, from antiquity to the modern day. In ancient times the idea was often written subtlety to reflect the sensitivities and power structures and cultural environments of the time. Throughout our life on this planet, humans have asked themselves and others the 'why are we here' question, and wrestled with the intuition that there was more to life than contained in the accepted scientific, historical and religious accounts of the day. For example, Carl Gustav Jung (1875-1961), the eminent Swiss psychiatrist, psychoanalyst and founder of analytical psychology, suggested that all the most powerful ideas in history go back to archetypes. He wrote: 'This is particularly true of religious ideas, but the central concepts of science, philosophy and ethics are no exception to this rule. In their present form they are variants of archetypal ideas, created by consciously applying and adapting these ideas to reality. For it is the function of consciousness not only to recognise and assimilate the external world through the gateway of the senses, but to translate into visible reality of the world within us.'[1] Jung also regarded dreams as communications from the unconscious, which might be couched in a symbolic language that was hard to understand, but were not necessarily concerned just with wishes, or ways of concealing the unacceptable. Most commonly, he suggested, dreams were compensatory to the conscious point of view—that is, they were expressions of aspects of the individual that were neglected or unrealised, or warnings of divergence from the individual's path (Storr, 1998). This example of a relatively recent science-based exploration of the individual's life purpose, which has been considered historically as a purely spiritual matter, or as the object of pseudoscientific study, is important to note, because it reflects a positive trend that is bringing science and spirituality together again, and the 're-membering' of the knowledge and connections that we hold intrinsically as a species, and which were very much in the daily purview of ancient civilisations, but we have forgotten.

3.1 Overview: the human experience construct

So, here we go …

- Existence itself is sentient. That is, it is intelligent, and it has design and purpose. There are no coincidences. Existence can also be thought of as the universe, or universes, universal energy, or a supreme God, or everything, or life force, or 'chi', or the many other expressions that have been used by different peoples at different times.
- The idea is that the universal life force has a desire to know and understand itself. It achieves this through the creation of entities that exist in a way that can enable self-exploration and ask the key probing questions. These entities can be con-

1 Collected Works, Volume 8

sidered as souls and their natural state as spirit. Our natural state is spirit. Physical human beings are an extension of their spiritual or higher selves. We are an artificial body created as a vessel for our spirit, and by extension for Existence to experience itself. Our three-dimensional universe provides an environment of challenge and thus growth through which Existence learns about itself.

- Our natural state is spirit. When we go to sleep, we return to that natural state. Our daily lives are the true dream state. There is no death as most humans consider it. Death is the ending of a human experience and can be considered as a return to spirit and a state of bliss. The apparent barrier between our three-dimensional experience and the spiritual world is often described as 'the veil' or 'duality'. In reality, human experience is an extension of our spiritual essence. We may have multiple human experiences in parallel, emanating from the same soul.

The human experience provides one of the greatest progressions and opportunities for growth because, at this moment in our time, our true nature, origin and purpose are not collectively understood or accepted. Therefore, from a position of ignorance of our source and nature, our first major challenge is to ignore the conscious collective acceptance of reality and explore the non-mainstream, but ancient, knowledge of the true nature of reality that existed in many cultures and in many places. Luckily, our scientific materialist paradigm is changing, and for children born on Planet Earth in the twenty-second century, it is unlikely that this will be part of their journey.

- Incarnation into the human experience is not random and is not coincidental. At a spiritual level, choice of time of birth (era), environment (location, family), personal and physical attributes (personality, health, gender, sexuality) and likely events and challenges (global, local, personal) are chosen to enable specific aspects of learning and growth in our lives. The circumstances and experiences of our formative years create a backstory or point of reference with which to view and consider others—in our vicinity, across the planet and eventually from other parts of the universe. I believe that the opportunity to consider and accept the differences between ourselves and others is a necessary part to achieving elements of most people's purpose as a human being, because real growth requires understanding and the actions of compassion and empathy.

- Souls incarnate together, to provide pre-arranged levels of support for each other's journeys and paths. Soul groups may incarnate together multiple times, playing different levels of support for each other. Awareness of this is often received through past life regression. Note, however, that some established past life regressionists have come to understand in recent years that reincarnation may not be linear. Rather, all events occur simultaneously. Therefore, the past life regression experience is actually tapping into connected souls in other parallel realities, not a past life that you have actually experienced. (See www.bashar.org for more)

3.2 Human experience paradigm: impact on practical spirituality and life purpose

Having chosen to incarnate into a human body, along with all the other creatures living a three-dimensional experience in our constructed universe, it can be said that the human experience is similar to the premise of the movie *The Matrix* (Wachowski, 1999), except that our natural state is spirit and we are not being used as batteries by intelligent machines. It follows that, because it was a conscious decision to be incarnated with a defined set of parameters (era, location, family, environment, challenges) our lives have purpose (see 3.9 for more detail).

As the greatest growth comes through challenging and overcoming adversity, in whatever form, it appears that finding out that there is a purpose and a plan is a challenge in itself, although one that most people do not realise or accept, or consider in an unconnected way. And that is before we consider the challenge of finding and fulfilling that purpose. Many people live their lives without realising that there is a purpose at all. In fact, there may be multiple purposes throughout our lives, and we may not be explicitly aware that we have one or what it is. Nevertheless, throughout our lives opportunities and decisions are presented that allow us to move towards achieving our purpose, should we desire it. These situations allow us to experience challenge, fear and risk. Although many people step forward to embrace these challenges and the rewards of working through them, many do not. Either of these outcomes, and the multiple outcomes between, are valid life experiences, as it is the journey and not the destination that is important.

The idea is that every life experience is valid, including *not* becoming aligned with a sense of purpose. We can learn from those experiences, on some level, perhaps at the end of this incarnation. We understand this at a subconscious level, which is why activities that achieve a meditative state are so important, because they allow us to consciously reconnect with our spirit and draw on the myriad sources of support available when we try to re-understand our reasons for incarnating and begin to work out how to deal with the challenges of life. The idea is that awareness of, and action towards, achieving our life purpose leads to greater alignment with our true (higher) self and ultimately brings us greater life fulfilment and happiness.

3.3 Fields of consciousness

What is consciousness? In early 2022, I became aware of the work of Dr Steven Greer, the founder of the Centre for the Study of Extra-terrestrial Intelligence (CSETI), on the understanding of consciousness and the ways it can be used to communicate with non-human intelligences in this and other dimensions. My interpretation of his work is that consciousness actually describes the way things are in our reality. How existence works. There's no magic, nothing divine, just the nuts and bolts of reality. However amazing we may perceive this to be, the idea is that basically it's how things work: that is, it is how intent can affect physical form, and the power of meditation to change thought and actions on an individual, global and cosmic level. This is the basis of the manifestation ideas. It is also the basis of the work of Paramhansa Yogananda, as articulated in his original work *The Science of Religion* (Yogananda, 1925) and referenced in his later work *The Autobiography of a Yogi* (Yogananda, 1946)

Dr Greer's mission is to establish peaceful and sustainable relations with extra-terrestrial life forms, to which end he has been researching the nature of reality and our engagement with non-human intelligent life for over fifty years. He has developed and disseminated the CE5 Protocol as a process to achieve this (available through the CE5 app). In his documentary *Close Encounters of the Fifth Kind* (CE5) (Mazzola & Greer, 2020), he discusses the science of consciousness and the unity state of consciousness that exists across all species across the universe. In an interview with Dr Edgar Mitchell, the sixth person to walk on the Moon, and founder of the Institute for Noetic Sciences (IONS), they explore the idea of 'field consciousness'.

> *I theorise that there is a spectrum of consciousness available to human beings. At one end is material consciousness. At the other end is what we call 'field consciousness', where a person is at one with the universe, perceiving the universe. Just by looking at our planet on the way back, I saw or felt a field consciousness state*
>
> —Dr Edgar Mitchell

The research draws on scientifically observed phenomena that lend themselves to the idea of universal consciousness as the bedrock of our reality. Greer suggests we tend to think of consciousness as 'this sort of amorphous, irrelevant, interesting but mystical thing, but that actually the central operating system and communication system for all interstellar civilisations is consciousness and thought, and technologies that interface with them'. He states that 'consciousness, this faculty of being sentient and awake, is not limited to our brain waves or bodies, but in fact transcends the limits of space–time, the unbounded field of awareness. It doesn't matter if you intellectualise it or not, that is the reality of it and it has been proven scientifically'. He makes reference to the work of Dr Robert Jahn (1930-2017), who was the dean of engineering at Princeton University and founder of the Princeton Engineering Anomalies Research Lab (PEARL), a parapsychology research programme that ran from 1979 to 2007. The team at PEARL was supported by Adam M Curry, inventor, entrepreneur and teenage 'thought challenger' on consciousness, who was himself influenced by Adrian David Nelson's *Origins of Consciousness: How the Search to Understand the Nature of Consciousness is Leading to a New View of Reality* (Nelson, 2016).

One of the projects undertaken at PEARL was an investigation into the mysterious ordering effect of consciousness on quantum systems, an effect the team called 'mind–matter interaction'. They explored the idea of a non-local account of consciousness and found that it does not seem to be produced by the brain alone; rather, it involves the brain, but there was something much deeper going on. In other words, consciousness may not be localised to our bodies, but may be a fundamental feature of the physical world in which we live in.

The universe looks less like a big machine than a big thought
—Dr Dean Radin
Chief scientist, Institute of Noetic Sciences

One of the PEARL team's most demonstrable experiments was the use of human intent through thought to influence a random number generator. This kind of generator can be thought of as a scientific coin flipper: it looks at something intrinsically random in the physical world, and converts it into a string of ones and zeros. Studies have shown that if you collect a large enough sample size, you find an equal distribution of ones and zeros, meaning physical reality is behaving in the way it should. However, the PEARL experiment found that if you put someone in front of the machine and you ask them to use their intention to shift the mean to more ones than zeros without any physical attachment to the machine, what you find is that often there is indeed a statistically significant shift in the direction of their intention. This simple experiment has profound implications because it suggests that consciousness does not seem to be a localised phenomenon, rather it has the ability to affect probabilities at the deepest layer of reality, at the basement layer of the quantum world. In the words of David Bohm, eminent theoretical physicist and pioneer of quantum theory: 'Mind and matter are not separate substances. Rather, they are different aspects of the one whole and unbroken movement.' (Bohm, 1980)

Expanding his explanation of non-locality, Greer suggests that 'in both physics and consciousness there is a connection that exists amongst all things, photons to people to awareness, that isn't limited by space and time per se, that is woven within each other'. He refers to a famous experiment by scientist Masaru Emoto (1943-2014) that used intent to influence water patterns, as documented in his book *The Hidden Messages in Water* (Emoto, 2004). The experiment used photography to show crystalline structures in the water that were heavily influenced by the mood and emotion of the intention directed at it. For instance, if there was a very negative intention, the crystals' pattern would be dissonant, but when the emotion was very conscious or loving, the crystals' structures would be beautiful and ordered. These experiments were repeated by other scientists. Greer suggests that water has a crystalline component, but it's also tied, like all matter in space and time in this universe, into this consciousness forcefield. If you enter into a quiet state of consciousness and intend something very positive, it literally alters the structure of the water itself. In the documentary *CE5*, physicist Dr Russell Targ points out that whilst Schrödinger explored non-locality and entanglement in the 1920s, the physicists Stuart Freedman and John Clauser at

Berkeley University 1970s discovered that entangled photons can move far away from one another, and if you grab one, you instantly determine the state of the other.

The total number of minds in the universe is one. In fact, consciousness is a singularity phasing within all beings
—Erwin Schrödinger
Nobel Prize winning physicist

Another intriguing unpublished experiment by the PEARL team involved a room with no windows containing a house plant that needed light to grow. The room had a single grow light mounted in the centre of the ceiling that could turn towards one of four quadrants. The direction was controlled by a random number generator, which meant that over time it would shine equally in all four directions. When the plant was placed in a corner of the room, researchers found that the light shone more often on its quadrant. It was suggested that life itself, even in something as simple as a house plant, bends probabilities in the direction of what it needs—that is, in the direction of growth and its evolution. A profound conclusion.

Everyone who is seriously interested in the pursuit of science becomes convinced that a spirit is manifest in the laws of the universe—a spirit vastly superior to man, and one in the face of which our modest powers must seem humble
—Albert Einstein

The notion of accessing the field of consciousness is not a new idea, although it is perhaps a forgotten one for most of humanity. The Buddha spoke in detail about how to quiet the mind and use meditative techniques to access the field of consciousness. This, he said, allowed one to see into the past and future, and provided diagnosis and healing. Religious traditions and science are today converging on this idea of universal consciousness. Meditation is the gateway through which we can know and experience this connection. Greer suggests that 'the whole universe is actually folded within every single conscious being, like a quantum hologram. If you look at it, every single sentient being in the cosmos has folded within the structure of its consciousness the entirety of the cosmos, which is why within these deep quiet meditative states you can obtain knowledge, see places, know things and communicate, because in reality it's always there, you just have to get into a quiet state of consciousness where it opens to you.'

Does thou reckon thyself only a puny form
when within thee the universe is folded?
—Bahá'í teachings

Greer explored meditation by studying the ancient Vedic text of India (see 4.1.3.1). He found that they contain an excellent articulation and explanation of consciousness, as well as the science of consciousness, higher states of consciousness and their effects, which are known as the Siddhis. These include the ability to levitate, teleport, dematerialise and rematerialise, bi-locate, tri-locate, go through solid objects and achieve precognition and telepathy. These are all things that develop spontaneously as you enter into deeper and higher states of consciousness. It is suggested that these abilities were and are available to everyone through the process of quietening the mind and achieving deep meditative states.

As we have learned, consciousness is not limited by space and time, so if you are conscious and awake, the entirety of the cosmos is folded within you like a quantum conscious hologram. So, to access this we need to go inside, to the deeper aspect of ourselves, and when we connect with it through deep meditation, we have reached the point where we can be an ambassador to the universe, because we have become universal (Mazzola & Greer, 2020).

What we conclude from these works is another example of the age-old idea that we are all connected. We tend to think that this comes from spiritual or religious sources and is somehow connected with faith or the mystical boundaries of religions; but now science is returning to the party after a few hundred years away and suggesting, and confirming, the same truth.

In the late 1990s, the Global Consciousness Project, directed by Roger Nelson of the Institute of Noetic Sciences, placed dozens of random number generators around the world and analysed their output to see if they could discover anything about global or collective consciousness. They found that 'when human consciousness becomes coherent, the behaviour of random systems may change. Random number generators produce completely unpredictable sequences of ones and zeros. But when great events synchronise the feelings of millions of people, the network of generators becomes subtly structured. We calculate one in a trillion odds that the effect is due to chance. The evidence suggests an emerging "noosphere" or the unifying field of consciousness described by sages in all cultures.' (Nelson 2009)

The project found that on 11 September 2001, a few hours before the first plane struck the North Tower of the World Trade Center, this network of random number generators became more coherent, less random, and the data went off the charts. Nelson and his team had been reviewing this data since the late 1990s. It showed similar global spikes related to other events, such as the 1997 death of Princess Diana, the 2000 crash of the Concorde airliner, the 2004 Madrid Train bombing, the 2005 funeral of John Paul II, and many more.

The *CE5* documentary suggests this shows a deep relationship between collective consciousness and the physical world. Social studies have shown that if a group of meditators go into a community, they can effect significant behavioural change through deep, directed meditation, even though they make up less than one per cent of the population. They found that accident and emergency room visits declined, as did violent crimes and other kinds of negative behaviours—even though it wasn't generally known that the meditators were in the city. This suggests there is a resonance effect, whereby the meditators influenced the tangled, interwoven field consciousness of those around them, causing them to become better ordered, more peaceful and generally happier. One inspiration for these studies was experiments in the field of quantum physics in which a container of helium was cooled to close to absolute zero. When one per cent of the helium was aligned coherently, the entire container went through a phased transition, instantly shifting into coherence and taking on almost magical properties—a state called of superfluidity. So there was a transformation at that 1% point. When a critical mass of people, whether 1%, or a fraction of that, depending on the state of consciousness of those who are practising the meditation, prayer or coherence, but at that point, you can shift an entire civilisation. We become aligned and coherent and move in the right direction, and this transforms the other ninety-nine per cent, even though they don't know that we are doing it.

The opportunity in this example is to maintain the exercise for long enough to shift the normal vibration of the critical mass of the population, who are not in meditation, leading to a permanent change of state. That is the beauty and the power of the structure of non-locality in consciousness. It is all interwoven, but there's enormous power when you are operating at that deeper level of consciousness. This offers enormous potential for humanity rapidly to evolve out of its current situation into a higher state of consciousness and a happier, more aligned life and planet. These points bear repetition. We are all connected and have always been. The challenge and opportunity for us as individuals and as a species is to access the tools available to us to maximise the benefit of this, for the greater good of everyone, our beautiful planet and existence itself, wherever in the cosmos that may be.

As I will expound throughout this book, from a practical spirituality perspective, **the 'go-to' action is always meditation**. Find the meditations that work for you. Start simply with guided meditations and breathwork to focus, and then expand. Learn, develop, go deeper and deeper still. And the deeper you go and more practice you do, the greater will be the wisdom and guidance that appears to you on what to do for your personal alignment with purpose and the greater good of all. Intent is key. Have a pure heart and a clearness of mind and heart, bring them into resonance together and invite the field of consciousness to make your connection with it evident. Then you can send out your positive intention of love, light and positivity through this universal network. Since I started running meditation classes, the transformational experience for the students has been amazing. I am humbled to be able to offer this to others. See 4.1 for more.

Information on the work of Steven Greer and the CE5 Protocol can be found through www.gaia.com and *Close Encounters of the Fifth Kind* was available to watch on Amazon Prime in 2022. Since its development and introduction in the 1970s, thousands of people using the CE5 Protocol have experienced thousands of peaceful engagements with extra-terrestrial beings, including face-to-face meetings and dialogue. Not surprisingly, most of the species they have engaged with have been significantly more advanced than we are, both technologically and in their awareness of reality and the universal field of consciousness. In some cases, species have been billions of years in advance of us, often meaning they have transcended the need for physical bodies and instead appear to us as forms of pure energy—almost what we might consider angelic in their appearance—but beings, nevertheless. This is a potential journey for humankind, but the first step is meditation, meditation, meditation! For more on consciousness check out *Initiation* by Matias de Stefano, also on Gaia.

As water by cooling and condensation becomes ice,
so thought by condensation assumes physical form.
Everything in the universe is thought in material form
—Paramahansa Yogananda
author of Autobiography of a Yogi

3.4 Living inside and outside the Matrix

The idea of living inside or outside the Matrix refers to a construct in which we can be present in the actions of our everyday lives (inside the Matrix), but can also step outside of that construct and observe ourselves being present in the Matrix from a somewhat external perspective. The reference is to the film of the same name, which presents us with what appears to be the contemporary Earth, but is actually a false reality created to stimulate our minds and our bodies to function under the control of an artificial intelligence (AI) in order to create power for it. Real human bodies, although fully grown, are kept in embryonic pods, with cables attached to feed them, create the mind-stimulating illusion of reality and extract the electrical power generated by the bodies. The movie takes us on the journey of the main protagonist, Neo, as he struggles to understand the true nature of reality and reconnect with his real body.

Before he makes the journey, he has to make a choice between taking a blue or a red pill: the blue option will allow him to remain cocooned in the Matrix, in contented ignorance; the red pill will make him aware of reality, through extraction from the pod and integration with the real humanity, however uncomfortable that may be.

In discussing the reality of our existence, I will often refer to this movie—not because I believe we are living in a computer-generated reality to feed an AI entity, but because of the idea of duality. I want to suggest that our apparent reality has been created, within the structure of existence by a God, or something like a God, to allow us to learn through adversity. We do this with a degree of ignorance about our actual reality, that is, our spiritual selves. So, duality is the idea that we exist both within the Matrix as our human selves, but also outside the Matrix as spirit.

The work, challenge and opportunity of practical spirituality within the human experience is to take both blue and red pills and become aware of the Matrix from inside and outside at the same time! Humankind has been trying to achieve this for millennia. It may have been called by other names—enlightenment, nirvana, oneness with God, ascension—but it is essentially the same idea: to break through the apparent veil separating our three-dimensional human lives from the spiritual realm, and benefit from conscious awareness of both, in parallel. I believe meditation is the tool we need to start to achieve this, and I believe the purpose of this awareness, for most of us, is not to escape to our spiritual selves forever, but to use it to help achieve the purpose of our human lives. By being inside the Matrix we are experiencing the real issues, challenges and joys of the human experience. By being outside, we are observing our response to all of these factors, and this supports our growth by helping us to work through the challenges.

All matter originates and exists only by virtue of a force which brings the particles of the atom to vibration. I must assume behind this force the existence of a conscious and intelligent mind. This mind is the Matrix of all matter

—Max Planck
Founder of quantum theory

Practical spirituality supports this level of dual awareness or consciousness, whereby you are aware from your spiritual level and of your human-level decisions, actions and feelings. The aim is to respond to, and learn from, both. This dual awareness helps you see and respond to the apparent realities of human experience from a different and sometimes removed perspective. From the point of view of human-to-human interactions, this enables greater empathy and compassion because objective observance allows you to consider the energy that is driving the thinking and actions of others. It also helps you not to take it too seriously, since you understand that ultimately it is all a construct. This does not take away the very real perception of pain that we experience in our human interactions and sometimes it is unfathomable that a situation would be created, by design, in which humans commit the most heinous acts against other humans.

I still find this hard to accept, even from my personal perspective of what the human experience is. It is certainly something very personal to reconcile the theory of this paradigm with the extremes of its reality, however great the opportunity for growth through healing may appear to be for victims of atrocities. The challenge to reconciling this is because it is driven by feelings rather than logic and intellect. For most of us, being aware of, or even witness to, heinous acts, in particular against other humans, usually triggers an emotional reaction on a deep level, reflecting the fact that we are feeling beings in a feeling universe.

No problem can be solved from the same level of consciousness that created it

—Albert Einstein

3.5 Time

We tend to think of time as linear. There is the past, which flowed into the present, which flows into the future. Many who work with past life regression consider multiple incarnations as part of a linear soul journey in which we learn the lessons from one life and go on to apply them in the next. An alternative suggestion is that there is no such thing as time, that time is a construct created for us in this three-dimensional paradigm in order to experience the process of managing the challenges that we attract in our lives. This suggestion goes farther to suggest that there is only one moment in all creation, sometimes called 'the eternal now', and that time is an illusion created by consciousness.

An analogy can be drawn with celluloid films … in a projector, the individual frames of the film are shown in a rapid, steady sequence of still frames that creates the illusion of flowing time. But in truth, the frames exist simultaneously. There is the illusion of time only when the frames flow through the projector. In fact, the projectionist can take out the roll of film, spread it out on the floor and view all those frames at the same time. The theory goes that in a similar manner, our consciousness projects individual frames of reality in a steady and extremely rapid sequence. Bashar says we do this billions of times a second, thus creating the illusion of the flow of time. Each of these individual 'still frames of reality' contains no motion whatsoever! It is a frozen snapshot—perfectly still. And yet, by sequencing these still frames we have the illusion of the flow of time. (Note: The actual 'frame-rate' for the physical dimension that we are experiencing is an extremely tiny interval, defined by Planck's constant).

From a practical spirituality perspective, what this means

to you and how you live your life as a result of believing it, or otherwise, is obviously very personal. I find it intriguing. I love trying to bend my mind around the idea that if I slowed everything down to multiple trillionths of a second, I would be able to observe a single frame of my three-dimensional existence. But then I love mind-bending concepts ... like the gravitational effect on time in the movie *Interstellar*, where one hour on Dr Miller's Planet equals seven years in the orbiting spacecraft!

Although I think it could be true that time is a product of consciousness, and I find the possibility fascinating, in terms of my daily life and my purpose it affects me only in the sense that I know and believe that time is malleable and everything is possible: that is, we can communicate with what we consider to be the past and future. In reiki energy healing, we connect to moments in time through energy, essentially following the principles that everything is energy and energy is not bound by space and time

3.6 Family and early years experiences: creating a point of reference

From my observance of life over the past fifty years, I believe that our family setting and early years are a crucial part of our purpose in life. That is the part of our lives when we are dependent on others to create the environment for the start of our human experience. This creates our point of reference, which gives us our perspective on life and others, framed in terms of nationality, values, culture, language, wealth, opportunity, social interaction, intelligence, compassion, gender and sexuality. These are the factors that make up the person we believe ourselves to be, and how we perceive and feel about ourselves and our world. As I've said, this is directed and planned before incarnation and birth in order to create an environment that will give us the opportunities we need to grow in the theme that we have chosen for this life in order to achieve our purpose or purposes. There are no coincidences.

Having established this point of reference by the time we reach our late teens, most people on Earth then have to work out how to engage with the world and in particular the 7.6 billion others who do not think the same as us and do not have the same point of reference. This then creates a massive opportunity for growth. In fact, through my life experience and my work on compassion-based mediation (CBM) it is my belief that the Planet Earth growth model (or Matrix) is based entirely on the idea that our biggest challenge in life is everyone else, and this alone provides ample opportunity for our souls to grow—which is the point of the human experience.

The written and oral history of humanity presents us as a species that has never stopped fighting and killing each other since the moment we could record our stories, essentially because we could not find the compassion and empathy and emotional intelligence to reconcile our points of reference with those of others. And that continues to this day, whether it be to address some sense of lack of power, or perceived threat, often motivated by our intolerance of others' beliefs, culture, religions, gender, colour, race, ideology, sexuality, history … and the list goes on. For me, this supports my belief that our human experience is intentionally set up in this way, to create a perfect environment for our souls to learn compassion and empathy. Unfortunately, here on Planet Earth, our report card is mostly taken up with 'plenty of room for improvement!' and 'could try harder!'

3.7 Ancient history and artefacts

Every ancient and native culture has embedded within its origin story the idea that they were created by another being of some sort, and that they were also given knowledge and shown how to develop in all aspects of their lives. These other beings came from the sky, then left when their work was complete.

This is one of the key tenets of the Ancient Astronaut Theory, first posited by the Swiss author Erich von Däniken in the book *Chariots of the Gods: Unsolved Mysteries of the Past* (Von Däniken, 1968). His work provides an explanation for identical structures that exist all over the world, for example the pyramids found in Egypt, Central America, China, Europe, Antartica and all over the world, as well as similar customs and beliefs that are found among ancient peoples, which conventional historical and archaeological theory cannot explain because these peoples, thousands of years ago, apparently had no way of contacting each other.

A large part of these unexplained similarities are connected with the stars. For instance, the three major pyramids of the Giza Plateau in Egypt align with the three stars in Orion's belt as they appeared in 12,000 BP (Bauval, 1989), as do major structures at Chichén Itzá in Mexico. All over Earth, humanity is continuing to discover ground-based drawings, or geoglyphs, that can be seen in their entirety only from the sky, but which were produced long before humanity apparently had access to flying machinery. Examples can be found in Peru (for example, in the Nazca Lines), India, Australia and many other places.

Some of these coincidences and mysteries have been brought to the public's attention by the TV show *Ancient Aliens*, produced by Prometheus Entertainment and shown on the History Channel since 2009. They raise the idea that our planet and its history and the true nature of our existence are populated by information and evidence that does not align with conventional thinking about the history of our species. This information is ancient, and much of it embedded in one of the few substances—rock—that can endure over long periods of time. Together, they hint at the existence of prior civilisations on Earth that had high intellect, advanced technology and spiritual awareness and connection with the stars and other sentient beings.

What does this mean for practical spirituality? In the early days of my awakening, because my process was led to a great extent by my reading of *The Only Planet of Choice*, I thought that the extra-terrestrial component of Earth and humanity's story was the key or the main story—almost to the extent of becoming obsessed by making contact with extra-terrestrial beings myself. I think this is probably quite common among people who have been gifted that level of revelation. However, as time and my journey have moved on, I have come to realise that, in general terms, the extra-terrestrial exists within our generated environment, our Matrix. Although other species no doubt have access to higher intelligence and technology, including the ability to bend time and space, travel interdimensionally, and even to exist in multiple planes—the physical, the spiritual and a combination of both—they nevertheless exist within the framework of an experience created for souls to grow and for existence itself to understand itself.

I believe that at the time of writing, in the year 2022, we are reaching a point in Earth's history when the public will gain more accurate knowledge and understanding of the true nature of our history and existence. This is often referred to as 'Full Disclosure' (when governments stop their covering-up activities) or 'First Contact' (the first public engagement with an alien entity). This journey started many years ago, but the process probably accelerated from the moment we detonated the first atomic bombs in the 1940s and sent a message out to the universe that our species had achieved the capacity to destroy itself. Researching and becoming aware of these issues, for example by exploring the idea of ancient aliens, is a good way to raise your consciousness to the level of a wider galactic and universal community and gain insight into a deeper and older human backstory.

Over the past decade we have seen greater public engagement with the topic of extra-terrestrials and UFOs by governments and retired military officials from the USA, Canada, France, UK, Chile, Russia and other countries. In 2021, the US government made an unprecedented reversal of its previous policy by admitting that it was aware that non-human entities visited Planet Earth, and had done for many years. A report prepared by the US Office of the Director of National Intelligence, dated 25 June 2021, titled 'Preliminary Assessment: Unidentified Aerial Phenomenon', stated that of 400 cases of such phenomena investigated in the USA between 2019 and 2021, only one could be explained as a human-created object. The other 399 remained unexplained.

The US government went on to suggest that visits by non-human entities represented a threat to the Earth and the US, rather than being a potentially amazing and beneficial opportunity for humanity to engage with our sisters and brothers from the cosmos. The fact that 'we are not alone' is fairly obvious for anyone, even if they are not aware that our galaxy contains a hundred-thousand-billion stars, and that the known universe has more than a hundred billion galaxies. According to NASA's Exoplanet exploration programme, our nearest exoplanet, Proxima Centauri B, is only four light years away.

'Exoplanet' is the term given to planets that appear to fit a human understanding of the parameters for the most likely ability to sustain life, including distance from the sun, gravity and orbit. A light year is the distance that light travels in a single Earth year (nearly 6 million miles). Therefore, travelling at the speed of light it would take an object four Earth years to get there from Earth, or vice versa. The vast distance is often the counter argument given by some traditional scientists and other less-expanded mindsets to the idea that intergalactic space travellers could have ever come to Earth. If, however, we expand our understanding of reality, as we explored in section 3.3, and we think outside of the box on the nature of the connection between space and time, as well as the potential use of technology to interface with reality, then what seems impossible starts to become very possible. A mobile phone transported through space and time to the fifteenth-century Earth would have seemed like magic. And yet, as we know, it is just technology.

From a purely statistical perspective, it is inconceivable that there is no other sentient life elsewhere. For me, this is a given. What isn't a given is how each planet in our situation, on becoming aware that they are not alone, becomes able to accept this. I am sure that on some planets the collective consciousness is awake and advanced enough to accept this, allowing the transition to be relatively smooth. Unfortunately, on Earth at the start of the twenty-first century, we are living through a fairly low level, all-too-human struggle in which the beneficiaries of the old paradigm are positioning themselves to control the transition in order to ensure they maintain and expand the levels of power they have been used to—especially since the Industrial Revolution. Space, interdimensional access and connection with thousands, if not billions, of other species is a massive opportunity from a power perspective, and these people hope to achieve their goals using the traditional control structures of governments, royal families, corporations and, most importantly, the global industrial complex. There is a multitude of information you can access about all of this—and I suggest you do. Get informed, form your own opinion about what is going on here on Planet Earth, then decide what you want to do about it.

I believe strongly that humankind will eventually move away from its fear-based, externalising paradigm and will accept the reality of its reality—that we are all individual, unique, empowered beings who have access to our higher self and the field of consciousness. Once we do this, we realise we do not need to rely on the individuals, systems and structures that we believed were supporting us, but which are actually controlling and 'dumbing down' our lives. From that point forward, humankind and Planet Earth's evolution will be exponential, almost to the point where we won't even remember how imprisoned we had allowed ourselves to be.

In the meantime, anything that stretches our consciousness makes a positive contribution to our ability to handle change, and possibly lead it, too. I believe this point may be the key to why you are reading this book right now. Your journey has taken you from the moment before your soul incarnated in your current body to the moment when this information is important to you and can support the achievement of your purpose.

I believe that we all chose to incarnate on Earth at this time, but we didn't come for an easy ride; we came because this is a tough gig, and therefore the growth potential for our souls is huge. We are born with no memory of our true selves, on a planet that is in the dark about so much of what reality really is. This means we are ignorant of the amazing opportunity that existence gives us. All we see is a planet consumed by violence and 'otherness' that is simultaneously developing the ability to build colonies on other planets, whilst new-born babies here on Earth are denied clean water, food and security, and the very concept of compassion for fellow human beings is sidelined, ignored, perhaps not even considered, in the drive for power and to satisfy ego, greed and material wealth, in its many forms. So, into this environment we have come, willingly (at a soul level), to try to remember why we are here and ultimately to make a difference in some way for the betterment of humanity and to help it move forward, into the light.

3.8 Religions

This is always an emotive subject, probably because religions dominate our planet and have affected so much of our development as a species, and not always positively. In the 1997 science fiction movie *Contact*, based on a 1985 novel by renowned astronomer Carl Sagan, the character of Dr Ellie Arroway is challenged to justify why she as a non-religious scientist should get the job of being the first and only human being to represent Planet Earth on a journey constructed by and to visit Earth's first extra-terrestrial contact, when 'ninety-five per cent of the population believes in a supreme being in one form or another'.

I love this film, partly because of the way the theme of

science versus religion plays out on many levels throughout it. In fact, as I said above, I think science and spirituality (to which religion is connected) are actually coming together. In the twenty-first century we are beginning to find that what was once considered myth or legend can be proven through the rigorous scientific method that has dominated, and often restricted, progress for so long. More on this in other chapters.

In a spirit of disclosure, I do not believe in a God in the traditional religious sense: that is, as an omnipotent old man. But I do believe in the power of the spirit of existence, whether you call it chi, universal energy, all that is, or the essence of existence. I believe Planet Earth and our three-dimensional universe to be a training ground, a school, a place for souls to come to grow. I also believe the Earth is suited to this purpose precisely because its population in general lacks knowledge and understanding of its heritage.

Many of us are effectively living in the dark about all aspects of why we are here and what our purpose is, and the purpose of existence in general. So, although the basic tenet of this school is that we should work stuff out ourselves, we are not doing so alone. We have at our elbow a realm of spiritual support, and always have had. In our understood history, we are aware of figures who appeared on Earth with messages about how to live our lives, what values we should strive to hold and the need to have compassion for others. It is my belief that messengers such as the Buddha, Jesus and Muhammad came to Earth to provide a course correction to the human species, guiding our development towards compassion, empathy, emotional intelligence and higher-level growth.

Now, it could be argued that this has been achieved on some level, as the religions that sprang from such interventions were based on concepts of compassion and treating others well. Unfortunately many of them—some to a greater level than others—have been corrupted by mankind's basic insecurities and its unenlightened perspective on the nature of existence, of which material greed and the desire for power are particularly dominant manifestations. It has been said that Jesus never intended for humanity to create a religion in his name. On a mass and almost industrial scale, this was the doing of some very Earth-bound followers, quite possibly with strategic goals that had little to do with compassion and the enlightenment of the species..

The basis of practical spirituality is that our individual connection to spirit and the divine essence of the universe is through ourselves, and not through some external deity or religious structure. We are unique souls, on a unique path, and we come to Earth with all the tools we need to reconnect spirituality with our divine inner and higher selves. We are inherently spiritual, we just don't always know it. Our God is inside us, because it is us, and we are it. We are a unique representation of all that is, a unique aspect of universal everythingness.

One use I and many others have found for religious places is to visit them to connect with the energy that is there. This is not because of their religious nature, but because more often than not they have been built on the sites of ancient high and special energy locations that were recognised as such by ancient peoples. These people, who are often referred to as pagans in Europe, or native peoples the world over, were connected spirituality with all aspects of their environment. So, these locations can sometimes provide a higher and perhaps easier connection with source energy and spirit guides.

3.9 Finding and living our life purpose(s)

So, what is a life purpose? Does everybody have one? As our discussion so far has shown, the answer to this question is: yes, everyone has one or more goals, and each will be unique to a given individual. These goals may change to reflect phases in a person's life. Undoubtedly my own purpose, which only became clear to me at fifty-two years of age, required that I undergo all the activities and challenges and opportunities and growth of my previous fifty-two years, in settings all over the world.

In many cases, the search for a purpose itself may be part of your purpose, because it will involve the inward exploration of the self that usually comes from it. Examples of purpose may be to experience being a leader, or a worker in a large organisation, or to get involved in helping others in some way, perhaps through charities or counselling. It may be to be a parent or a carer in some way, to win the National Lottery and deal with the challenges that that creates. Sometimes major events such as winning a lottery may just be the enabler, rather than the purpose itself. The purpose in this case may be to learn to deal compassionately with the extensive demands that come from having extreme wealth.

Many people pursue the idea of bliss in this incarnation, sometimes referred to as nirvana, or a conscious reconnection with a higher self while in their three-dimensional existence. This journey of discovery may be your purpose. Personally, with my logical head on, and with absolute respect for the validity of all experiences, I think bliss is our normal spiritual state, and we incarnate into this experience in order to learn and grow through the challenges of this limited state. Therefore, I doubt that, for most of us, the point of our time here is to try to reach some spiritual bliss state … but again, every experience is valid.

Exploring this further, there is an idea that in the same way that we as individuals explore our purpose and grow through raising our vibration, so does the planet. The idea of third-density beings living on a third-density planet, and through a process of raising their vibration evolving into fourth-density beings on a fourth-density planet is an ancient concept, explored by many, and articulated in texts such as Thomas Vazhakunnathu's *Spiritual Theory of Everything* (Vazhakunnathu, 2020). Vazhakunnathu suggests that this is the normal evolution of existence itself, as planets are conscious and spiritual entities in their own right, but directly connected to their inhabitants and the events of the cosmos. He suggests that every evolving density is of a higher vibration than the previous one and is less dense. For beings, this may mean that as they evolve, they become physically less restricted, to a point where they no longer require any form of physical body. Eventually, beings return to existence itself, as pure, formless energy.

From the practical spirituality perspective, what does having a purpose mean? And does it matter? For me, it mattered because I was searching for a purpose for so long and after quite a few diversions, I finally landed on something that felt right. This gave my life direction and allowed me quite naturally to make decisions about my actions and responses to opportunities as they arose. The criterion I applied was: does this opportunity align with my purpose? If yes, proceed; if not, do not proceed.

Now, although this sounds fantastically simple, it isn't always that clear cut—but it does provide me with a framework within which to live my life. The reiki master Jim Pathfinder Ewing suggests that 'it is our role in life, our soul's purpose, to order energy and reality to suit our higher purpose, as co-creators with the Creator. This is the power of being, with its imperative to use this power to help bring order and harmony to this world'. (Pathfinder Ewing, 2011). So, if you have this sense of knowing and feeling that what you are doing right now resonates with a deeply felt sense of who you are … then keep doing it. If you can say it is your highest excitement, then you are probably in an aligned place. If, however, you have a strong sense that there is something else, then chapter four presents twelve steps, tools and techniques to help the ideas crystallise and come to the fore and may even allow the universe and synchronicity to work its magic.

3.10 Human experience: a summary

Before we begin our exploration of practical spirituality's tools and techniques, it might be a good moment to pause and give a summary of what we have learned of the human experience in this chapter.

- The universe is conscious, and has a desire to understand itself.
- Souls and spirits are a manifestation of existence itself and are the normal status of existence.
- Human 'being' is a manifestation of the universe through spirit's quest to understand itself through the creation of the physical three-dimensional experience we know as life on Earth.
- It is no coincidence that our lives have challenges.
- Nothing is real.
- Through challenge comes the opportunity for understand-

ing and growth. And to understand compassion through action.

- Everything is energy. Energy is everything.
- Everything exists now. There is no past or future.
- Everything is an opportunity. All that matters is how you respond.
- You have an amazing support team.
- We should strive to be open and aware.
- Be true to your own uniqueness.

3.11 Practical spirituality: what is it?

I define practical spirituality as living your spiritual and life journey within the daily life challenges of work, travel, home, family, finances and the rest. It could be considered in terms of what you do every day, every week, every month, every year. It is a matter of deciding what your life's spiritual plan or journey might look like, and how you strike a balance between those responsibilities and activities that support your spiritual growth and aspirations. These might include actions such as:

- Meditation practice
- Being mindful
- Developing healthy sleep patterns
- Eating a healthy diet
- Following an exercise regime
- Engaging in spiritually uplifting entertainment
- Learning and growing
- Spending time with people who've had enlightening experiences
- Being in nature
- Pushing your spiritual boundaries
- Journaling for reflection and planning

- Being conscious of your thoughts and feelings
- Attending retreats
- Consciously working towards your life purpose
- Being 'present'
- Stepping outside of yourself
- Being aware of your duality
- Giving back
- Supporting the raising of human consciousness on Planet Earth
- Being compassionate and empathetic
- Recognising and living in abundance
- Combining your spiritual with your personal interests
- Considering how to combine your spiritual interests with achieving satisfaction and progression in your job
- Considering and mastering how to deal with being the only spiritual person in your family, social circle and work group
- Balancing your spiritual journey with rest of your life
- Being spiritual despite getting rich.

Chapter four explores all of these approaches in detail to provide guidance on steps that we can all take to achieve these goals of spiritual balance with everyday life. My approach is based on my experience of living through the frustrations of trying to combine family responsibilities and challenging careers all over the world with a burning desire to explore my spiritual journey, develop my spiritual practice and ultimately discover and live my life purpose.

4: Twelve practical tools and techniques to raise your vibration, find your purpose and embrace your spiritual aspirations

The underlying purpose of all of these tools and techniques is to raise your vibration. Anything that shifts you, even slightly, from your normal self and removes the clutter of everyday life from your mind can only be positive. At the very least you will feel slightly better, and at most, you will increase your connection with your higher self and the realm of universal possibility, as well as the spiritual assistance that is constantly available to support you in your life's journey.

As explained in the previous chapter, there are twelve steps because of the numerological power of this number. I believe it has inter-universal and interdimensional significance, and thus actions taken within the concept of the power of twelve have the potential to reach far beyond this world and are supported by concepts and forces greater than those we as humans can comprehend at this stage of our evolution.

I believe that all these tools and techniques raise the vibration of your consciousness and so contribute to achieving a life more aligned with your true purpose and therefore increase your fulfilment and happiness. **The only way to find out if this is true for you is to take action** … Oh, and why not keep a journal as you do, then you can look back to see how this journey has changed your life. Have fun!

At the end of most of the Twelve Steps sections, there is a real life story of practical spirituality. I am honoured to have been given these by friends, family and colleagues who resonated with the idea that everyday practical spirituality could assist them and inspire others. I am extremely grateful to the authors, and feel blessed by their amazing stories and the courage and commitment they showed in writing them down.

The twelve steps are:

1 Meditation and quiet reflection
2 Moving your energy (through exercise, diet, sex)
3 Giving back by embracing a more compassionate life for yourself and others
4 Following your flow—be true to yourself, learn to trust your gut/intuition and higher self
5 Change the way you think (declutter, stretch, do things that are different, explore thinking differently). Do things that are spiritually uplifting (that make you smile)
6 Learn to be present, improve your dreaming and explore altered states
7 Think and reflect … but most of all TAKE ACTION
8 Increase your awareness of your true past and your reality … inside and outside the Matrix
9 Explore the idea of your true-life purpose and alignment with your truth
10 Consciously manage your time.
11 Explore energy healing
12 Visit special 'energy places'.

4.1 Meditation and quiet reflection

Meditation is the key to removing blockages and opening the doorways to our spiritual selves. In this section, we explore the benefits and history of meditation, the challenges we face and techniques for overcoming them. We finish with Suzanne's story, which tells how she discovered she was able to enter a meditative state—'in flow' or 'in the zone'—through painting.

Meditating and getting into a meditative state (for example, by using breathing, or walking barefoot in nature) is a great way to clear out the day-to-day clutter and reconnect and align with our higher selves. Through meditation, we have the potential to improve flow in the conduit between our earthly conscious state and our spiritual state, allowing guidance and assistance to come through in a clearer way. You could even, whilst in a meditative state, with an attitude of gratitude, simply ask a question, such as 'What is my purpose?' or 'Can you show me what my purpose is?'

Getting into a meditative state regularly—ideally, daily—and being mindful of messages and signs and opportunities coming back to you, puts your daily life in a higher state of consciousness (or higher vibration) and improves your ability to deal with the lows and blows and confounding confusions and painful experiences that life sometimes throws at you.

4.1.1 Definition of meditation

Meditation practice has existed on the planet for thousands of years, with the earliest recorded mentions in the ancient Sanskrit texts known as the Vedas, written some 4,000 years ago. Subsequently, meditation played a salient role in the contemplative repertoires of Hinduism and Buddhism. Most indigenous peoples on Planet Earth have a way of creating altered states, a feature of meditation that is integral to their human life experience and is used for healing and connecting with higher states of consciousness.

Meditation is defined in many ways, among them:

- A state in which the body is relaxed, the mind is quiet and we are alive to the sensations of the moment' (Harrison, 1993).
- 'The first object of meditation is to become the master of your mind' (Long, 1995).
- The Dalai Lama comments: 'Whatever forms of meditation you practise, the most important point is to apply mindfulness continuously, and make a sustained effort. It is unrealistic to expect results from meditation within a short period of time. What is required is continual sustained effort.'
- Meditation creates a calmer state of mind and may significantly reduce stress, anxiety, depression and pain, and enhance peace, perception, self-conception and well-being.
- Meditation can heal using natural energy.
- It can be a religious practice (for example, by incorporating prayer) and may be a type of mindfulness.
- Meditation is a practice where an individual uses a technique—such as mindfulness, or focusing the mind on a particular object, thought, or activity—to train attention and awareness and achieve a clear, calm and stable mental and emotional state.
- 'Meditation isn't about becoming a different person, a new person, or even a better person. It's about training in awareness and getting a healthy sense of perspective. You're not trying to turn off your thoughts or feelings. You're learning to observe them without judgment. And eventually, you may start to better understand them as well' (Headspace, 2021).

Scholars have found meditation elusive to define, as practices vary between traditions and within them. Meditation is practised in numerous religious traditions. Since the nineteenth century, Asian meditative techniques have spread to other cultures where they have also found application in non-spiritual contexts, such as business and health. Research is ongoing to better understand the effects of meditation on health, whether psychological, neurological, or cardiovascular, and other areas.

4.1.2 Meditation to connect with higher consciousness

For me to describe meditation and its importance and significance to practical spirituality, we need to explore the human experience (see chapter 3), and I have to describe the conclusions, drawn from my personal experience over the past fifty years, of what that is.

In many ancient cultures the human experience is described in terms of souls or spiritual beings incarnated here on Earth in order to have human experiences.

> *This is the crux of what it means to be a spiritual being having a human incarnation: to discover, accept and express our inheritance of oneness with the source and channel its essence of excellence as we deliver our gifts, talents and skills in the world*
>
> Dr Michael Beckwith

Exploring this further, we find the idea that our natural state is spirit, and that we have a higher self—our true spiritual self, if you like. In the spiritual realm we have access to all-knowing, all-existence, in a space where there is no time or space, just being.

Our human incarnation, the thing we generally think of as ourselves, is a representation of our true selves, incarnated in this somewhat limited three-dimensional environment of the Earth in order for our spirit and soul to grow through the challenges and thus opportunity that life brings us, or which we attract. The themes of our lives are pre-planned, and thus the conditions of our birth (where, when and who to, the environment, etc) are not random or coincidental. They are part of a complex fabric of arrangements created so that we might have the opportunities to grow by dealing with the challenges they present us with.

Many people believe that their existence is a solitary one and they must survive their lives alone. This could not be further from the truth. The spiritual environment that facilitated our birth remains in place to support us throughout our life, but we tend not to notice. Unless we ask for help, only extreme situations, in which we are seriously off-track with our life themes and purpose, will stimulate an unrequested intervention, whether through serious medical emergencies, out of body experiences, near-death experiences or the like. The purpose of these is to kick-start us back to alignment with our purpose, which often happens to people after they undergo that kind of episode—for example, they may become more compassionate, focus more on their health and the feelings of those around them.

We live on a planet of free will and choice (Schlemmer & Jenkins) and so the spiritual environment can only present us with opportunities; it cannot force us to take action. At the same time, for many of us, life can be confusing and even those following a 'spiritual path' find this to be the case. I believe the reason is because the growth of spirit and soul comes from the challenge of working through confusion. And because of the density of the world in which we live in today, we are disconnected from natural and spiritual energy in a way that our ancestors were not. This can make it feel like there is a layer of heavy blankets around us, blocking us from our spiritual selves and the extensive and immense amount of support available to us … if we ask for it.

Luckily, we have meditation. I think of meditation as the key to opening the doorways to our spiritual selves. I describe meditation, in the broadest sense, as anything that takes us out of our three-dimensional human mind-space and opens our awareness to a greater state of consciousness. Let's face it, most of those on Planet Earth today spend most of their lives dominated by their minds, and stimulants that target their minds (TV shows, movies, news, advertising, social media and the rest). This is very dense energy and we need meditation to break down the apparent barriers between our three-dimensional life experience and our 'normal' spiritual state. This reduces density, and at the very least, helps to create calm and stillness and enables a more peaceful life. At the greatest, it facilitates stronger connection with a conscious, sentient universe that exists to enable us to live our highest, greatest good.

With this approach it is important to remember that:

- Nothing is truly real
- Everything is an opportunity. All that matters is how you respond …
- You have an amazing support team
- You should be open to and aware of what might appear in your life (synchronicity/manifestation)
- Be true to your unique self
- Meditation can help create greater understanding, a feeling of reality and an awareness of our own path.

4.1.3 A history of meditation

The Vedas

The earliest written record of meditation is in the Vedas, in particular the Atharvaveda, produced in what is known as the Vedic period, the late bronze age/early iron age, approximately 3500-2500 BP. These are believed to be some of the earliest comprehensive texts on Earth, and are presented in four chapters: the Rig Veda (the oldest, written between 3800 BP and 3100 BP), followed by the Yajurveda, Samaveda and the Atharvaveda (produced between 3200 BP and 2800 BP).

'Veda' means knowledge in Sanskrit, and this is presented in two forms: words and objects. Veda in verbal form is contained in Mantra, and other literature. Veda in the form of objects refers to the whole universe, that is, the objects in the universe are denoted by 'Veda', or the meaning of the word is reflected in, or represented by, the whole universe (Thakar, 2010). Together, they form the basis of the Hindu religion, but they have contributed their wisdom to other belief systems, including Buddhism. The Veda are considered to be 'sruti', which means 'what is heard', to distinguish them from religious texts called 'smriti', or 'what is remembered'.

Hindus consider the Vedas to be 'apaurusheya', a word that can be interpreted as meaning 'not of man', 'superhuman and impersonal' and 'authorless'. It originated in the revelation of sacred sounds and texts heard by sages after intense meditation. This lends itself to the idea of universal knowledge as something that 'just is'. By tapping into the knowledge-bank of existence (or field consciousness) through meditative processes, we can all access this information and improve our understanding and our experience of our human lives.

The four Vedas contain details of life during this period that have been interpreted to be historical and have the following focuses:

- **Rigveda (3800-3100 BP)** This mainly contains various hymns for praying to Vedic Gods such as Agni (god of fire), Indra (lord of the heavens), Varuna (god of water), Surya (the sun god) and many more. These hymns are called riks, hence the Veda is called Rik-Veda or Rigveda. It has 1,028 hymns and 10,600 verses.
- **Samaveda (3200-2800 BP)** This is the Veda of melodies and chants. It is a liturgical text, relating to formal public worship and consists of 1,549 verses, all but 75 of which have been taken from the Rigveda. The Samaveda is said to be the root of much of the music and dance tradition on this planet (Beck, 1993).
- **Yajurveda (3100-2800 BP)** Yarjus means 'worship' in Sanskrit and the Yarjuveda deals with prose mantras and worship rituals. It is a compilation of fomulas for ritual offerings that were spoken by a priest while an individual performed ritual actions such as those of the Jayna fire (Witzel, 2003). The earliest and most ancient layer of the Yarveda Samhita (collection) includes about 1,875 verses that are distinct yet borrow and build upon the foundation of verses in Rigveda.
- **Atharvaveda (3000-2800 BP)** This is the knowledge storehouse containing the procedures of everyday life. It is a collection of 730 hymns, with about 6,000 mantras divided into twenty books (Bloomfield, 1899). About a sixth of the Atharvaveda texts adapt verses from the Rigveda; most of the text is in verse form and deals with a diversity of Vedic matters. The Atharvaveda is described by some as the 'Veda of magical formulas' (Patton, 2004). In contrast to the hieratic, or

priestly, religion of the other three Vedas, the Atharvaveda is said to represent popular religion, and incorporates not only formulas for magic, but also the daily rituals for initiation into learning (upanayana), marriage and funerals. Royal rituals and duties of the court priests are also included.

The Atharvaveda addresses a wide variety of issues, including the use of mantras for teaching and meditation on spiritual knowledge, speculations on the nature of man, good and evil, medical remedies, good health practices such as yoga, prayers for peace, the science of higher knowledge, the idea of a single Vedic god, states of consciousness, the existence and nature of the soul, among others. It is from the Atharvaveda that most currently practised forms of Vedic-based yoga and meditation originate, for example Ayurvedic and Kriya (see Self-Realization Fellowship, www.yogananda.org).

Each Veda is divided into four subdivisions, namely:

- Samhitas: mantras and benedictions
- Aranyakas: text on rituals, ceremonies, sacrifices and symbolic sacrifices
- Brahmanas: commentary on rituals, ceremony and sacrifices
- Upanishads: texts discussing meditation, philosophy and spiritual knowledge.

Sometimes a fifth is included: the Upasanas, which deal with worship.

The early Upanishads were composed between 2900 BP and 2300 BP, whereas the others, including a number with greater familiarity in modern times, were produced later. The chronological order is as follows:

- Mahabharata
- Bhagavad Gita
- Ramayana

- Samkhya Sutra
- Mimamsa Sutra
- Arthashastra
- Nyaya Sutra
- Vaisheshika Sutra
- Yoga Sutras of Patanjali
- Brahma Sutra
- Purana
- Shiva Sutras
- Abhinavabharati
- Yoga Vasistha

Modern day

Over the past seventy years, meditation has gone from something 'Eastern', espoused by Western 'hippies or alternative folk', especially in US and European-based cultures, to something that is practised by millions of 'ordinary' people all over the world and is now even encouraged by the corporate world to support their staff. Research suggests that some of the most notable people in history, including Albert Einstein, Nikola Tesla and possibly even Leonardo da Vinci, used meditation or the exploration of altered mental states to relax and to seek inspiration.

As we have seen, meditation has a history stretching over thousands of years, and so there are many ways and means available. The key is to find something that works for you. There are many resources available through the internet and the mind, body and spirit sections of bookshops, as well through support from spiritual life coaches.

As a reiki healer and teacher, I find that meditation focused on the rebalancing of the chakras is the most beneficial for me, and I make it part of my daily practice. I have also explored meditative and trance experiences that are more 'journey based', with a defined purpose of discovery. Shaman-led quests, for example, can help you to tap into knowledge that you are ready for. The use of plant medicine, including ayahuasca, also has the potential to facilitate a meditative journeying experience. You can read more about ayahuasca in Ralph Metzner's *Sacred Vine of Spirits* (Metzner, 2006).

4.1.4 Types of meditation

In general, there are two categories of meditation: passive or dynamic, although some, such as sophrology, combine both (Sophrology Academy, 2021). There is no right way or wrong way to do it, so look for the ones that resonate with you. It is important to be clear that for most people the process of calming the mind and establishing a regular daily practice is not easy. This is why perhaps it is called a practice—because you have to keep practising. But the benefits of making it part of your daily routine, even if only for twenty-to-thirty minutes a day, can be life-changing over the longer term, particularly in reducing stress and enabling healthier approaches to the challenges of everyday life.

I believe meditation is essential to practical spirituality. Many techniques are aligned with certain yoga practices, which have their origin in the structure and intention of the Vedas (see above). Of the multitude of meditation techniques that have evolved over the past 4,000 years, I have picked out a few approaches in the list below to illustrate some of the differences between them, and to suggest their specific benefits and applications

Passive meditation techniques[2]

Mindfulness

These originate from Buddhist teachings and pay attention to thought without judgment. The aim is simply to observe and take note of patterns. It combines concentration with awareness, and may be useful to focus on an object or on breathing while observing bodily sensations, thoughts and feelings.

Spiritual

These are used in religions such as Hinduisma and Christianity, and is similar to prayer. The idea is to reflect on the silence around you and seek deeper connection with your God or universe. Essential oils such as frankincense, myrrh, sage, cedar and sandalwood are sometimes used to heighten the experience. They are beneficial for those who thrive in silence and seek spiritual growth

Mantra

This is prominent in many teachings, including Hindu and Buddhist traditions. It uses repetitive sounds to clear the mind, such as the word 'Om'. It increases alertness and connection with the environment, and leads to deeper levels of awareness. Beneficial if you don't like silence and enjoy repetition.

Focused

These use concentration on any of the five senses. This may be an internal technique, based on breathing, or external, such as counting mala beads, listening to a gong, or staring at a candle flame. They may suit those requiring additional focus in their life.

2 For more information check out www.headspace.com

Transcendental

This uses a mantra, or series of words that are specific to the practitioner. It benefits those who like structure and are serious about maintaining a meditation practice

Progressive relaxation

Also known as body scan meditation, this is a practice aimed at reducing tension in the body and promoting relaxation. It often involves toughening and relaxing one muscle group at a time, or imagining a gentle wave flowing through the body. It sometimes focuses on chakras and is beneficial to unwind and relieve stress before bedtime.

Loving-kindness

Used to strengthen feelings of compassion, kindness and acceptance toward oneself and others. It typically involves opening the mind to receive love from others and then send a series of well wishes to loved ones, friends, acquaintances and all living beings. It benefits those holding feelings of anger or resentment.

Visualisation

The aim here is to focus on enhancing feelings of relaxation, peace and calmness by visualising positive scenes or images. Important to imagine the scene vividly and use all five senses to add as much detail as possible. A variation is imagining yourself succeeding at specific goals to increase focus and motivation. It is often used by elite sports people; it boosts mood, reduces stress and promotes inner peace.

Sound bath

Uses bowls, gongs and other instruments to create sounds that help focus the mind and bring it into a more relaxed state

Vipassana

Taught by the Buddha as a universal remedy for life's ills. It aims at the eradication of mental impurities and achieving the highest happiness of full liberation. Vipassana ('to see things as they really are') is a way of self-transformation through self-observation. It focuses on the interconnection between mind and body that can be experienced directly by disciplined attention to the physical sensations that form the life of the body, and continuously interconnect and condition the life of the mind. It is this observation-based, self-exploratory journey to the common root of mind and body that dissolves mental impurity, resulting in a balanced mind full of love and compassion. Usually taught in ten-day retreats, with a strict code of conduct.[3]

3 https://www.dhamma.org/en/about/vipassana

Chakra balancing

Chakra means 'energy centre' in Sanskrit. Each centre is associated with a specific organ, issue, emotion, colour and element. Balancing these centres can have physical, emotional and spiritual benefits.

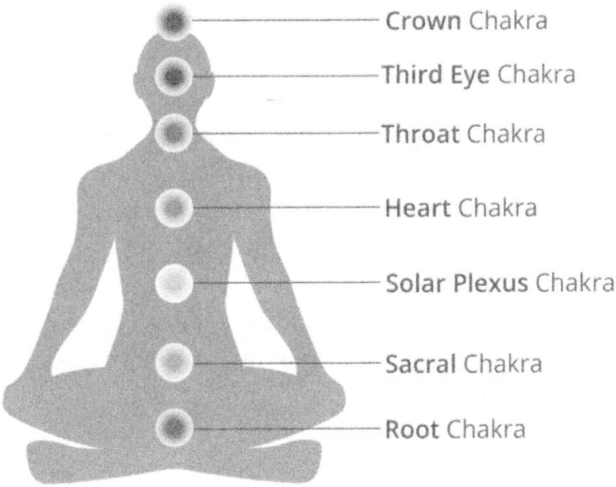

Dynamic meditation, requiring movement

These techniques use rhythmic and repetitive movement to achieve an alternate state, for example through walk and dance and body movements such as yoga. They have their origins in Osho's 'Rajneesh Dhyan Yoga', developed in India. Examples include:

- Sama and Hadra among the Sufi mystics
- Gurdjieff movements, in the Dynamic Body Awareness (Conscience corporelle dynamique or Consapevolezza cor-

porea dinamica)

- Other sacred dances, Qigong and the many exercises developed in Buddhism and Taoism
- Tai Chi, an ancient Chinese discipline of meditative movements practised as a system of exercises
- In India, those found in Yoga and Tantra, and the Latihan of Subud.

We often find that through mindfully walking along a beach, or being present while walking through the countryside, or dancing to a repetitive beat, we can achieve a meditative state. Shamanic drumming uses these principles to quieten the mind and shift our energetic focus to a deeper level. Check out ecstatic dance, 5 Rhythms and numerous online and face-to-face locations where dynamic meditation practice is available.

Quiet reflection

Our lives are typically busy and noisy with distractions from so many areas, not least from our mobile phones, as well the constant stream of messages, adverts and emails in the environments we pass through. The decision to respond to these immediately is a choice, in the same way as keeping your TV or radio on all the time is a choice. Many people are afraid of peace and quiet, sometimes because they worry about where their thoughts might take them. I am guessing that if you are reading this book, you are already open to the variety of places that your mind might wander without any external distraction, and hopefully you will find many techniques and approaches in this book to help you to process those thoughts into a positive space.

Quiet reflection is important to help you achieve a practical spiritual life, because it helps to remove the clutter of everyday life, much of which does not really serve your higher good or purpose. Even if it is not meditation, taking the time to sit in quiet, be it in your living space, outside on a beach, in the countryside, or on a river bank is important. The aim is to allow your thoughts to arise and pass on,

By acknowledging all the clutter that fills our awareness, and letting it go with love, you create the space to reduce your stress and allow more inspiration and more enjoyable thoughts to emerge. It may even happen that you find answers to challenges you are facing, for instance, a way to look at an issue that helps you to resolve it, or perhaps consider it from a different perspective. Taking the time for quiet reflection also contributes to self-compassion or self-love. The idea here is to look after yourself, or give yourself a break. This is covered more in later sections.

Suzanne's story

In the flow

When I am painting, I am all in—from getting out my paints, setting up the easel, taping the paper to my board, selecting my brushes, filling my jar with water, mixing my paints in the palette, sketching an outline, to the very first brush stroke. I enter a different world—a world of shades, texture, blending, wet-in-wet painting, brush strokes, a lift-out brush for highlights, rigger brushes for detail, fan brushes for foliage like dry grasses, grey paint for shadow, a world of ratios of water to paint. And whilst the technicalities are finite and controlled, the effects are sublime and flow—warm light from a cottage doorway, the glassy surface of a lake, the reflection of a bridge in water, the roundness of a lighthouse, the hues of a sunset. All these are things I derive pleasure from in the 'real' world, from nature; being able to recreate them brings me true joy.

So, what is it that touches me so deeply, and why? In watercolour, there is artistry in getting the shades just right, in the subtle touch or twist of the brush and there is magic too—in the tips and tricks that create a three-dimensional illusion. Quite simply, it is fun. However, there is more to it than just this. When I paint, I am finally in touch with a true part of me: the creative aspect of my personality is allowed to surface and breathe and I can just breathe, create and be … me.

Most of my fifty-seven years so far have been firmly attached to the physicality of life, dedicated to the business of working, raising a child and making ends meet. To be fair, all that commitment has led me to a fair few places in the world, living and working in the Far East, the Middle East and southern Africa. It has given me a wealth of experiences of different languages, culture and landscapes, which have without doubt enriched my life.

Along the way, life has tested me too, as it does us all, challenging me with the experience of being a single mum, financial insecurity, loneliness and depression. My desperation to find a way out/forward has led me on my journey to greater consciousness on a well-worn path of mind, body and spirit literature, starting with an interest in past lives, reincarnation, meditation, tai chi, reiki, angels, channelling, soul groups, crystals, aligning chakras. However, I have to admit that whilst I do feel more aware of this other dimension of life as energy,

I know that I have not yet committed myself whole-heartedly to this knowledge and so I guess I feel 'on the outside', an observer rather than a participant. What keeps me from committing? No doubt some of you will have an idea! Fear? Fear of failure? A deep-rooted fear based on past disappointments, that what is for others is not for me—that I will gather the courage, listen to the advice I give my daughter and students—to grab the bull by the horns, feel the fear and do it anyway, and dive in … only to find that the gates are shut. I am not allowed into the party. That it's not my party to go to. Is mine another path, though? I don't know.

However, when I paint, I am in that energy without thinking about it. I am present. It feels like a meditative state. It allows me to shake off the rigours and restraints of my physical life and experience life through the colour and shapes of nature. I am immersed in nature in the 'recreation' of it. Connected. And when I finish, I am relaxed and re-energised. An interesting consequence of this is an alternative way of perceiving what I see from the perspective of colour and shape. A cloud is no longer just a cloud—it can also be a combination of whites, creams, golds, pinks, purples, blues and greys in a myriad of shades. How wondrous is nature! And this discovery leads me to gaze longer, enquire more deeply, experience more acutely in the moment.

Coincidently (ha, ha) my work life has recently taken me to a place full of people who are artists, creators, writers. Having given up on getting subliminal messages through to me, has the universe simply pushed me into this arena—into the party? I am keenly aware of a creative energy embodied in the ethos of where I work, both past and present, since art and creativity are an intrinsic part of the history of the place. I am in the middle of a vibrant positive vibe. I am part of that. I am on the inside. Surrounded by people who make and create, I find myself inspired to pursue this new area of my life—my creativity—because it represents something in me that has been dormant for too long. A small part of me is in mourning for all the time lost, but more importantly most of me is happy and excited to be tapping into an energy source that is helping to paint the picture of who I really am.

4.2 Move your energy: regular exercise and a healthy diet

In this section we explore the importance of physical movement and appropriate diet to support good energy flows through and around your body, and to support positive mental health. David's story explores his spiritual journey and the importance of sport and good exercise to maintaining balance in his life.

4.2.1 Physical activity

Exercise daily

It has long been established that daily exercise has benefits for our physical, mental and social state. A 2019 British Medical Association report titled *Get a Move On: Steps to Increase Physical Activity Levels in the UK* (BMA, 2019) states that meeting the recommended level of physical activity can achieve the benefits shown in the list below.

Physical health

- Prevent or manage more than twenty chronic conditions

and diseases, including cancer, stroke and type two diabetes.

- Maintain a healthy weight[4] and reduce or prevent obesity (although it is important to note that the relationship between physical activity and obesity is complex and physical activity alone cannot prevent obesity).
- Maintain or improve musculoskeletal strength, supporting healthy ageing and reducing the chance of falls for older people. For example, physical activity can reduce the likelihood of hip fractures by up to sixty-eight per cent.

Mental

- Reduces the risk of, and manages depression, stress and anxiety
- Can increase motivation, drive and self-confidence. People who are inactive have, on average, three times the rate of moderate to severe depression as active people.

Social

- Provides opportunities for interaction, builds stronger communities and reduces isolation.
- Provides positive societal benefits. For example, participation in sport has been associated with increased educational attainment and reduced crime rates.

Even after a relatively short run of twenty minutes, I experience a positive mood shift that may last for days. This leads to a shift in perspective that can make issues that appeared weighty and unmovable seem less important, and often I find

4 A body mass index of between 18.5 and 24.9 is considered healthy. Although exercise is an important factor in maintaining a healthy weight, over-exercise can be damaging for health, and can lead to individuals being under a healthy weight.

a new solution to them. I walk for at least an hour every day, usually to the sea, which offers its own uplifting element; most weekends I walk in the nearby hills and venture further afield to mountainous areas when I can. Over the past few years, I have focused on running 10k races, which requires me to train three days a week. All of this is incredibly important, not only for my physical health and life expectancy, but for my mental and spiritual health. Not unlike meditation, running and exercise allow me clear out the baggage and garbage that occupies my mind on a daily basis and create space for inspirational and spiritual guidance and wisdom to become visible.

In addition to running and walking in the mountains, in my forties I learned to sail dinghys and then 35ft yachts in Wellington, New Zealand. I have continued this off the UK's south coast in more recent years. Active sailing can be physical work and achieves similar altered states as other forms of exercise.

Sailing and mountain walking are part of the 'active retreats' that Consciousness Awaken will be running, both from the south coast of England and on the Mediterranean coast near Barcelona. These events include yoga, meditation and personal spiritual development in a small group setting over a three-to-four-day period.

Walk in nature

Most of us are intuitively aware of the value of direct contact with nature. If, during your walk, you can strip off and do it naked—and sing and dance, too—then the contact is even better! Seriously, though, we have to be respectful of those around us and local laws, but being with nature, in woods and open fields, away from the dense energy of masses of other people, with at least our feet naked, is getting pretty close to a direct connection with Mother Earth, Gaia, Pacha Mama and the natural spiritual energy of our environment. This can only be positive.

It is also good to create the space for quiet meditation and reflection in these spaces, and be open to what happens next. Ancient woodlands are great for this, and some of my favourite spots are listed later in this book, including Kingley Vale near Chichester in West Sussex, the ancient and spiritual town of Glastonbury in Somerset, and the Wiltshire locations of Avebury, West Kennet Long Barrow and Stonehenge.

Swimming in the sea, especially naked, can also create that fantastic raw and honest connection with nature. Humans are the only creatures on Earth that have to create our own clothes and body protection, and we are also the species with the greatest disconnection from nature. The two are undoubtedly connected.

So, get out into your local woods, hills and meadows, embrace the sheer natural power and beauty of the sea, get out to your nearest mountains and take a wonderful, mindful walk across your nearest field—and don't forget to take your shoes off, if you can.

Regular sex

It is well documented that a positive, active and healthy sex life can support practical spirituality. It reduces physiological and emotional stress and increases happiness and intimacy with a partner. It can also be a way of exploring sensual energy through kundalini work, tantric massage and tantric sex. In addition, studies have shown other health benefits, including:

- Lower blood pressure

- Better immune system
- Better heart health, possibly including lower risk of heart disease
- Improved self-esteem
- Decreased depression and anxiety
- Increased libido
- Immediate, natural pain relief
- Better sleep.

Gayatri from Tantra Massage Training UK describes tantric touch as 'a path to awakening and experiencing our life-force energy, otherwise known as sexual energy, connecting sex, heart and spirit'. The existence of this ancient and powerful sexual spiritual energy is explored in more detail in *The Magdalen Manuscript* (Kenyon & Sion, 2002) and *The Sophia Code* (Ra, 2016).

It is my view that sex was included in the design of human beings for far more than ensuring the continuation of the species. The exploration of sensual and sexual energy has the potential to help raise our vibration and support alignment with our higher self and purpose. Sensual massage embodies the human need to touch and be touched, with the benefit of exploring sensuality and sexuality, which have the energy-enhancing benefits mentioned above. This does not have to mean sexual intercourse. Tantric massage in particular allows the recipient to explore the idea of receiving, with no expectations of giving, and for the giver to explore the idea of giving for its own sake. In our current societies these are surprisingly tough challenges for many people, and they provide an avenue along which we can explore the nature of relationships, and thus the nature of self. These are vibration-lifting experiences.

Eat healthily

'You are what you eat'! A well-known expression, and if you've been conscious over your life of the effect that has on you, you will be aware that it often makes you sluggish, tired, takes a long time to digest, or has even made you feel ill—or guilty. The answer is to stop eating food that has a negative impact on you.

There are multiple resources available on the internet and in bookshops to guide you to tasty, nutritional foods, so go and search. Remember that keeping it light and choosing a more plant-based diet is probably better than the opposite. I'm not currently a vegetarian, but I have been for long periods of my life. I'm aware of the differences in my physical and mental health when I eat what I would call heavy meats such as beef, so I pretty much avoid them. I tend to keep the meat intake to chicken, fish, and an occasional cheeky bacon butty ... because they taste so good. Otherwise, sticking to a mainly vegetarian diet can be fun, varied and help to keep your on-board food processing effective and efficient, without needing too many 'January detoxes' (although these are a good idea).

There are quite a few people who run courses on healthy eating, and you can combine these with with yoga, meditation and exercise, so explore things that resonates with you, your lifestyle, your budget and the time available to you for food preparation and management. I followed a keto programme in 2020 with Michael Mosely, combined with a running programme, which was tough but effective. I felt better and healthier and achieved my goals of losing 10 kg and reducing my body mass index to an acceptable level.

Remember to enjoy the process. Eating is a central part of our lives, so it's important to find a good, healthy regime that you enjoy—otherwise it becomes a chore and that has a less positive energy signature for you and your mental health.

David's Story
My spiritual journey

What is your earliest memory of spiritual awakening?

I was brought up in a fairly normal middle-class environment in a rural village in southeast England with one brother and two sisters—I was the second child of four. I was eager to please—a relatively gifted child who was pushed into musical development, with some sporting and academic talents and a private school education with church on a Sunday. I remember being a bit of a deep thinker even at an early age (and an active dream life established itself early on) but other than this there were no particular traumas or otherworldly experiences.

Private school led to university to study law (mainly because I couldn't decide what I wanted to do and law seemed 'useful'). In my final summer I spent two months in USA (Camp America), which initiated a love of travel and new experiences, and this then led, the following summer, to being taken on as a holiday rep working for one of the larger tour operators, which combined two of my long-lasting life interests—travel and people.

It was not until I returned from working overseas (winter and summer seasons) five years later (aged 27) that I experienced my first stirrings of 'awakening'. I particularly remember one night around the time my beloved Nana died that I experienced a 'peace that passes all understanding'—like liquid gold. Time had no meaning, I didn't know whether I was asleep or awake, but I knew I wanted to stay in this state forever. In the morning the intense loving feeling was gone but the memory remained

What happened next?

Around this time I found myself being drawn to the mind, body, spirit section of bookshops and a succession of what would become classics jumped out at me—Neale Donald Walsch's *Conversations with God*, Eckhart Tolle's *The Power of Now*, Diana Cooper's *A Little Light on Angels* to name but a few. This then led on to experiential workshops with some of these authors and others, and experiencing some of the energetic foundations and synchronicities that would continue to guide me.

By this time I had met my girlfriend, soon to be wife, and although the truth is that although I struggled with the mental gymnastics of committing to one person with all that entails for life 'till death do us part', I knew that we had a really good thing going with lots of shared interests and passion and it was nothing that a few sessions of reiki—another recent discovery—couldn't solve.

Experiencing and offering various modalities of healing and exploration into mediumship (much with my wife) led on to discovering the enigma that is crop circles and an energetic download experience aged thirty-three, which turned many of my previous certainties on its head and exposed me to the idea that there is much more to this universe than I suspected, including past/alternative lives. At this stage I needed some strong support and thankfully once I learned to ask, I received it from a number of different angles (including the invisible realms). I believe it is true that we are looked after and loved beyond measure.

Another key moment?

It took another couple of years to regain my energetic balance and although my everyday life continued much as before. I had moved on in my career to local government health and safety, and my wife and I decided to adopt two children following difficulties with conception. We even started attending a Methodist church when we moved house (partly to give our adopted children a solid Christian upbringing), but I continued with my alternative spiritual development (2012 and ascension theories/earth grid and galactic energies/multidimensional and lightbody development) alongside and things seemed to generally slot into place. That was all until the age of forty-four, when the wheels came off the bus.

It's hard to know exactly what happened and what caused what, but I had been experimenting with a combination of high-vibration spirituality and essence practices and the result was a full-blown mental health crisis. I don't want to spend very long dissecting this four-year period of my life (I have been forced to live in the moment), but it would be fair to say that it was a pretty intense dark night of the soul, and internally everything felt like it was being rearranged without my being in control although, strangely, some of my best understandings have come from this time in my life—particularly the realisation that life goes on however bad things feel, and you do matter in the grand scheme of things. Interestingly, my outer world remains much the same and many people other than my immediate family don't really know that anything happened.

Thankfully much of this is in the past (or rather does not impact unduly on my present or via my dreams, which remain a barometer of how things are going and where I'm at spiritually), but I retain a regular psychotherapy session as part of a healthy proactive mental health regime, alongside attending a men's circle, which is where I met Tony.

So what have I learned?

To build energy (or should we say 'love')?

a) I have returned to music (singing, in particular, makes me feel connected to my core self, and I can be brought to tears by beautiful and spiritual harmonies—maybe memories of other dimensions).

b) I understand that meaningful communication is a core soul-need in me having suffered a stammer in early childhood—I spent six years in a toastmasters' (public speaking) group, which gave me an opportunity to further hone communication skills and to practise telling some of my life stories to a limited audience.

c) My day job includes elements of training and I thrive on the ability to simplify complicated concepts and grow confidence in my teams—health, safety and wellbeing really are common sense—just do it!

d) Meditation and mindfulness—just spending time in the present—nothing formal, just time walking, sitting, or standing with the aim, simply, of holding the peace.

To shift energy

a) Running has always been a passion of mine—Parkrun 5k is my current vehicle but I have run on and off for many years (including a London Marathon and several Great South Runs). I guess it's always been about grounding, alongside all the other benefits.

b) Movement remains important—yoga, pilates, tai chi, dancing, stretching—I have tried them all but my favourite is yoga—it just seems to cover all the bases. That doesn't stop me having a dance around the living room on a regular basis.

c) Sport. Although these days it tends to be viewing rather than playing, I just love the way that sport transcends all differences and cultures, and some of my favourite life experiences have involved witnessing excellence, teamwork and transcendence in sport.

d) Travel. What used to be a general and work-related passion for travel (there's always something to learn about yourself) morphed into sacred travel for a period (Peru/Egypt/Australia/New Zealand/US/Canada) and has now changed again into walking holidays (Camino de Santiago/South Downs Way/St Cuthbert's Way, with other routes in planning).

To expand energy

a) I have been very lucky with my family (and dog)—always supportive, always looking out for each other. The children have been a test for us (whose aren't?) but even in my worst times I have never been tempted to give up on them.

b) Community. Whether it's a spiritual community or a work community, there is always somebody to connect with and I am truly grateful for all the wonderful people I have met over the years.

c) Service to others. It's a fairly new one on me, although my wife does this perfectly. I have only recently discovered how much of my life I have spent with a slightly introverted and navel-gazing perspective—higher vibration spiritual experiences tend to reflect that back to you so plenty of room for improvement there!

Final thoughts

a) Explore your world—travel, driving, walking, spending time with others—a healthy interest in anything that expands your body, mind and soul is good.

b) Every day is an opportunity—not necessarily to do or gain more stuff but to practise new ways of loving and being.

c) Time spent in nature is never wasted.

d) Gratitude for anything and everything is a wonderful way to start the day—much better than reading the news.

e) Be open to change—the universe will always self-regulate to direct you back to truth.

4.3 Embrace a more compassionate life

In this section we explore the importance of compassion for self and others, and the incredible power of laughter. These can raise your vibration and lead to a more balanced life. Sheila's story shares some major life challenges she faced. She describes the life-changing consequences of caring for herself and her needs, and how this allowed her to care for others, too.

4.3.1 Compassion: Treat yourself and others well

The essence of compassion, as described by Paul Gilbert in *The Compassionate Mind* (Gilbert, 2009), is basic kindness, with a deep awareness of the suffering of oneself and of other living things, coupled with the wish and effort to relieve it. He goes on to suggest that although most religions recognise its power, it was within the Eastern traditions, especially Mahayana Buddhism, the school of the Dalai Lama, that exercises and mental practices were developed to train the mind in compassion. In these traditions, developing compassion is like playing a musical instrument: it is a skill that can be enhanced with dedicated practice. This research also suggests that these traditions portray the development of compassion as having far-reaching consequences in terms of how the mind organises itself, how we experience ourselves and the world, and even the ultimate reality of our sense of self.

A definition of self-compassion is captured succinctly by the following words: 'When we are mindful of our struggles and respond to ourselves with compassion, kindness and support in times of difficulty, things start to change. We can learn to embrace ourselves and our lives despite inner and outer imperfections and provide ourselves with the strength needed to thrive.' (Neff & Germer, 2018) This work also suggests that research has shown that 'individuals who are more self-compassionate tend to have greater happiness, life satisfaction and motivation, better relationships and physical health, and less anxiety and depression'.

"Compassion is to be passionate about something, that is the origin of the word." So says Matias De Stefano (De Stefano, 2021). "So, share the passion of creation; share the happiness of creation. Christianity suggests compassion is to help others, but others are a projection of yourself, so the only way you can help others is if you are in your core, in your balance, and you are coherent with yourself. Then, by your act of being just you, you are sharing that passion with others, so others can wake up, see that you are fine because you are in the centre. Compassion is to share how you feel about yourself, about your balance." Check out his work through the GAIA channel.

4.3.2 Laughter

Most of us are aware of the expression 'laughter is the best medicine', and most of us will have experienced the changes in physical and emotional state that arise when we laugh. The more we laugh, the more we change and the better we generally seem to feel, whilst our mind and body appear to be brought back into balance. Laughter changes our perspective on a situation, even when it's at its direst. A quick internet search will bring up multiple sites explaining the science behind this, and many will highlight multiple benefits, such as strengthening your immune system, boosting mood, diminishing pain and protecting from the effects of stress. It lightens your burdens, inspires hope and connects you to others. It also keeps you grounded, focused and alert, and helps to release anger and forgiveness sooner that would otherwise be the case.

The mental health charity Help Guide International suggests that with so much power to heal and renew, the ability to laugh easily and frequently is a tremendous resource for surmounting problems, enhancing relationships, and supporting physical and emotional health. Best of all, this priceless medicine is fun, free and easy to use. As children, we used to laugh hundreds of times a day; as adults, life tends to be more serious and laughter more infrequent. But by seeking out more opportunities for humour and laughter you can improve your emotional health, strengthen your relationships, find greater happiness and even add years to your life.

The benefits of laughter and humour

Physical health benefits:

- Boosts immunity
- Lowers stress hormones
- Decreases pain
- Relaxes muscles
- Prevents heart disease

Mental health benefits

- Adds joy and zest to life
- Eases anxiety and tension
- Relieves stress
- Improves mood
- Strengthens resilience

Social benefits

- Strengthens relationships
- Attracts others to us
- Enhances teamwork

- Helps defuse conflict
- Promotes group bonding

The guide above summarises the benefits of laughter and humour for physical and mental health and the society as a whole. Further study has shown the beneficial mechanisms stimulated by laughter:

- It relaxes the whole body. A good, hearty laugh relieves physical tension and stress, leaving your muscles relaxed for up to forty-five minutes.
- Laughter boosts the immune system by decreasing stress hormones and increasing immune cells and infection-fighting antibodies, thus improving your resistance to disease.
- Laughter triggers the release of endorphins, the body's natural feel-good chemicals. Endorphins promote an overall sense of well-being and can temporarily relieve pain.
- Laughter protects the heart by improving the functioning of blood vessels and increasing blood flow, which can help protect you against a heart attack and other cardiovascular problems.
- Laughter burns calories. Although it is not a replacement for going to the gym or a regular running or exercise regime, one study found that laughing for ten-to-fifteen minutes a day can burn approximately forty calories—which could be enough to lose three or four pounds over the course of a year.
- Laughter lightens anger's heavy load. Nothing diffuses anger and conflict faster than a shared laugh. Looking at the funny side can put problems into perspective and enable you to move on from confrontations without holding onto bitterness or resentment.
- Laughter may even help you to live longer. A study in Norway found that people with a strong sense of humour

outlived those who did not laugh as much. The difference was particularly notable for those battling cancer.

And in summary, it's important not to take life too seriously or even your spiritual journey. I think we are given laughter in our human toolkit for a reason, and since it's fun, we should take full advantage of it.

A few suggestions for how to increase laughter in your life:

- Spend time with family and friends whom you know will make you laugh, and vice versa.
- Watch TV shows and films that make you laugh (don't watch the news!).
- Go to a comedy show.
- If you have young people in your life, especially toddlers, spend time with them … laughter and play is a major part of their day … go be silly, smile and laugh.
- Write down everything you took too seriously in life and tell a (smiley) confidante what you think about what good that did you. That ought to make you both laugh.
- Reminisce with a trusted friend about your biggest embarrassments growing up.
- Dress up in silly clothes.
- Look at pictures of what you were wearing ten, twenty and thirty years ago.
- Go dancing with positive friends.
- Hold a three-legged race with friends and family.
- Watch old family movies and view old family photos with family.
- Join a laughter group. Check out, for instance, the Hamlin Centre Laughter Club in the UK (https://hamblincentre.org.uk/laughter-club).

Sheila's story

My sense of spirituality is dynamic

I feel I am a light-bearer incarnated on this earth with the purpose of spreading the importance of faith, healing and love. On a microscopic level, I feel that I have been born into a family with many challenges and suffering, not only to help them spiritually, but to also grow and continually elevate myself to a higher level, closer to God. On a much bigger level, my spirituality includes a deep connection to music, education and philanthropy; it seeks to combine all religions into one universal stream towards the light force.

Being born into a Hindu family, I was naturally raised in a very spiritual environment where prayer and puja (service) to the Hindu gods was a daily custom. I remember being taught the Gayatri mantra at a very young age (I must have been around three or four years old), told to chant it every evening before going to sleep, and if I ever felt I had fears or doubts, this prayer would instantly fill me with strength. In addition to this there was the Hanuman Chalisa, which is a prayer to Lord Hanuman, who removes any negative energies and obstacles around you. He is known as the ultimate protector, and just thinking about him would always make me feel as though his presence was close by. This was like a foundation I had, surrounded by prayer and an invisible sense of protection. There were many moments during my childhood where I remember 'feeling' protected, although my actual awakening came years later …

Looking back, I realise that in my late teens and

twenties, I began getting into toxic cycles of falling into destructive relationships, which in turn zapped my confidence and had a knock-on effect on my health. Everything around me felt negative, including the toxic job I had as a headhunter, where I was exploited and mistreated. One day I woke up, unable to walk. It was frightening at the time because it came with waves of feeling like there was a brick banging against my head. It was also confusing to see and feel inflamed lymph nodes, the size of marbles, on the right side of my neck; amidst the worry, I was taken to hospital, misdiagnosed and discharged. However, my condition got worse, and the day after I was taken back and kept there. There were doctors all around me, prodding me, taking blood samples and trying to figure out what was wrong. All I felt was physical discomfort, pain and confusion. I was only twenty-seven. Despite the tears around me, with family members visiting me almost as if they were saying their goodbyes, I had a sense of knowing that I was going to be okay, even though physically I looked very weak—so weak, in fact, that I had to be carried to the bathroom. Other conditions emerged like a rash all over my body and feet, but I didn't give up hope that I would get better. On day seven, the lead consultant made a decision to do a biopsy to remove one of the lumps from my neck.

It was only after this biopsy that my symptoms begin to improve. A couple of days later, I was diagnosed with a rare autoimmune condition called 'Kikuchi disease'. When I learned that my immune system had basically given up on me because of the way I'd treated it, I had a complete shift in my consciousness. I realised that my awakening was stemming from this lowest point where I almost lost my life, and had to reconnect to my purpose, childhood dreams and ultimately, love. After being discharged on day ten, I spent a month at home, quit my job, and went back to pursue education—an MA in linguistics at University College London. That changed my life as it opened my world to private tutoring, which is my business now, more than a decade later! I also left the relationship I was in, which was like coming out of a cage … slowly, I began surrounding myself with higher vibrations, including a new circle of friends. I took up yoga and began treating my body with the respect it was craving …

Shortly after graduating, I went to Trinidad and Tobago for my friend's wedding. Whilst on a private hotel beach in Tobago, the hotel manager approached me to ask me what book I was reading. To be honest, it was just one I'd picked up from the hotel library and it wasn't stimulating at all. He literally took a book out of his back pocket and said, 'You need to read this book. It will change your life!' It was *The Power of your Subconscious Mind* by Joseph Murphy. It was the manager's book, but he said I could borrow it for the remaining three days of my stay.

This was my true life-changing moment because it introduced me to the power of our subconscious and also made me realise how the disease that hospitalised me had come about. From then on it was like a domino effect. I was drawn to spiritual books and gurus like Wayne Dyer and Deepak Chopra, sometimes introduced to me through random conversations with acquaintances or friends ... Every part of my soul resonated with what was happening because I was attracting those frequencies. It was as though higher beings were communicating with me with messages.

Then came reiki, introduced in a passing conversation. My hairdresser told me of a lady who was from Leicestershire but at the time was in London visiting relatives. She was a reiki healer and this fascinated me as I'd heard of this healing method but had not looked into it. I went to see her for a healing session and what I experienced in this session was nothing short of miraculous! As she did reiki on me, my hands literally began moving 'by themselves'. I had surrendered to this beautiful energy which was flowing through me and it was so liberating. It was fascinating, especially the way I felt as though I was walking on air just after the session. At that moment, I was so curious about what it was that I decided to book a one-to-one two-day reiki level one and two class with her that coming weekend. It was an addictive sense of being in a spiritual vacuum, and all the events leading to this moment suddenly made sense to me.

Shortly after this moment, I went on to do a seven-day NLP (neuro-linguistic programming) practitioner course with Richard Bandler, which was also transformative. Being a linguist, I was naturally drawn to this. Ultimately, I wanted to combine spirituality with scientific knowledge about the brain's wiring to be better equipped, and also help my own students. In 2020 I felt it was time to do the reiki master and teacher course, which couldn't have come at a better time. It has helped me, my family and my students during the Covid crisis, and has helped me feel closer to my guides.

Currently, my spiritual day looks positive and consistent. I meditate every single day without fail; I listen to Spotify playlists that have been put together for morning and evening mediations. Some of these include compositions by Ben Leinbach, the soothing voices of Krishna Das, Deva Premal and Tina Malia. I also practise yoga daily, most commonly the sun salutation—even if I have a busy schedule, I try and fit in five-to-ten minutes of yoga, and whenever possible chant mantras like the Gayatri mantra, the Buddhist *om so hum* and a number of others. I also regularly use frankincense and lavender carrier oils in my diffuser to ensure that my environment is full of good energies; on days where I feel particularly weighed down, I also take salt baths to cleanse and reinvigorate my body and mind. As part of my spiritual practice, I ensure I read something spiritual every day. Currently, I'm reading *Spiritual Warrior 1* by Bhakti Tirtha Swami, and I aim to read all six books of this collection.

Right now, I feel stronger and more focused than ever on my life goals. I look back at my earlier life as a necessary process, which was full of hurdles and countless obstacles, but led me to where I am now. I feel that my suffering and experiences will, one day, help others on an even bigger scale than they are doing now; I am constantly growing and learning with an open mind because I feel that knowledge is power when used to help improve the welfare of people. With an open mind,

I am able to draw in more beautiful conversations, experiences and special moments with like-minded people.

I've learned that human experience is not naturally designed to be spiritual, as we are sensory beings; however, nothing in life makes sense if we only look at our lives from this perspective, since then we would be like zombies, controlled by our false egos, and that angle would mean we are only born into a random body for sensory experiences—this is not true. We are fortunate souls to be born in the human form, and despite the challenges of practical spirituality in the modern world, it is necessary for humanity to understand that our health, wellbeing, mind-set as well as the love we feel and emit, are all interwoven with spiritual practices.

I've learned that it is necessary to take small steps in the 'right' direction; in my view and experiences, God gives us signs and it is up to us to follow these signs, but being idle and complacent will only stagnate our growth. In addition, there is a reason for everything that happens—where we are today is entirely based on our thoughts, choices and actions. Being objective in any conflicting situation helps to resolve any differences and feeling grateful is one of the most uplifting forces, capable of lifting anybody out of the darkest of places. Ultimately, there is no better feeling in the world than in giving to others. Whether it's a compliment, knowledge, a physical gift or kind words of wisdom, these acts of kindness can go such a long way, spreading like waves through the ethereal atmosphere whilst filling your soul with warmth and happiness.

4.4 Follow your flow—be true to yourself, learn to trust your intuition and higher self

In this section, we explore the importance of looking inside for 'you', quietening thinking and replacing it with feeling into who you are. Nige describes some of his own life challenges and shares with us how his inner focus, curiosity and connection continues to support his spiritual exploration and growth.

4.4.1 Explore everything that interests you

Entering a high state of passion is a key way to raise your vibration and align more closely with your higher self and guides. When we are passionate, excited and happy about what we are doing, we alter our state of consciousness, and the vibration of energy created by it is extremely powerful. It facilitates more positive doorways, pathways and resonances with your true self and your purpose, because it reflects an aspect of who you truly are. So, exploring sparks of interests to their full extent is important, particularly when you have no expectation of the outcome. The passion and excitement may be temporary, but that is okay because it is not meant to last: we have that learning, that growth and a great time, then we move on to other experiences. Throughout this process, you are learning more about what you do like and what interests you, and at the same time you will also be finding things that don't excite you, which helps to narrow your focus on your true purpose.

4.4.2 Read, read, read

There is so much knowledge out there. Even with Amazon and the easy availability of online material, it is still possible to go into bookshops and just allow the right book at that time to shout: 'Pick me! Pick me!' That has been my approach for the past thirty years, and sometimes it has led to what appeared like obscure works, but all had a lesson and a positive experience for me to enjoy, and some led to the further exploration of topics or authors that I had never considered. The bibliography of this book is based on these experiences, and most have been chosen from 'feeling'. I am sure you can do the same from a list of books on Amazon or elsewhere. Get down to Glastonbury, and get lost in the the Speaking Tree bookshop (www.speakingtree.co.uk) on the high street. This is an absolute must for every trip I make to the town, and a superb place for inspiration. Here you can allow the books you resonate with, and are ready for, to say 'hi'—if you relax and open yourself up to guidance.

4.4.3 Watch inspirational movies

The energy of inspirational movies has the ability to raise your own vibration and inspire you to take action. Great movies like *Arrival* (2016), *Interstellar* (2014), *The Secret* (2006), *Michael* (1996), *Close Encounters of the Fifth Kind* (2020), *Close Encounters of the Third Kind* (1977) among others. They have the ability to expand your perception of reality, which in turn expands your consciousness and signals to the universe and your higher self that you are ready and able to consider different paradigms. This inherently has a higher vibration and aligns with exploring and accepting the idea of an expanded view of what is possible, not only for the universe and existence, but importantly for you personally. By doing this you create an improved environment to receive ideas and maybe clarifications about what your highest excitement and purpose could be in this life time.

4.4.4 Travel to inspiring places

Without doubt, travel takes you out of your norms and comforts and expands your consciousness. The further you travel from your normal life, the more you will be expanded, as long as you remain open to embracing whatever weird and wonderful experiences come your way. Anything that contributes to this positive shift in consciousness supports your alignment with your higher self and purpose. Travel does not necessarily have to be overseas and exotic. For me, visiting natural energy locations is important. I go to Glastonbury Tor as often as possible and spend time in the town and visiting the nearby Chalice Gardens and the White Spring. The energy field there is important for my own 'recharge and reconnection'. Other important energy places nearby are Avebury, West Kennet Long Barrow and Stonehenge. Beyond the UK, there are multiple locations all over the world that hold special energy and provide a place for human reconnecting. There is a list of these in chapter six, but I would like to mention here the town of Sedona in Arizona and Mount Shasta in California. Anywhere where there is a history of ancient people's presence (anything more than 2,000 years), is likely to be a special energy place, because the ancients were connected at the most fundamental level with the natural energy of this planet, the universe and existence itself. So, visit these places, and be open to giving and receiving whatever you need to receive there, without expectation. What needs to happen will happen, even if you are not immediately aware of it at the time. Chapter six provides a non-exhaustive list of special places all over the world that are known to facilitate engagement with higher sources.

From a practical spirituality perspective, visiting these places is important because it expands your consciousness, not just through the engagement with the energy in the specific locations, but more broadly through the act of travel away from your usual environment. The opportunity to experience a different culture and physical environment is itself nurturing and expansive for our souls.

When visiting these places, I believe it is important to go with positive and open intent, with gratitude and humility. I was taught by a good shaman friend of mine to always ask to enter, with respect and then wait for a response. I think it is good to be present with the environment, ideally with limited expectations, prepared to offer something and be open to what you might receive.

This may not be anything, or at least anything apparent at the time. It is always a good idea to call in your spirit guides to assist and protect, if required. If you don't think you know them by name, then calling in Buddha, Muhammad, Jesus, Michael, Gabriel and other known positive entities is always a good idea. Using expressions like 'I call in spirits whose intention is of the highest good and value to support me' can be useful.

Nige's Story

I am a spiritual being within a human body. I am on a journey to experience creation in the human form, to experience as much as possible through the senses, emotions and feelings that I have been given. I believe that there is something for me to learn from this experience, something that I am here to do, a purpose to work with others in the relief of their suffering and trauma and to reach a place of spiritual connection and enlightenment.

I felt that I was somehow different from those around me when I was growing up. I didn't relate to a lot of things that I was taught at school and by family, but assumed they must be true. I toed the line and did my best but never felt truly connected with my peers or the teachings from my schooling and technical education. Science was our family paradigm; anything that couldn't be explained by science was considered fiction, this included all religious, spiritual and paranormal beliefs.

It's difficult for me to pinpoint my first experience of spirituality or of an awakening as there was no defined *ah-ha* moment for me. I have always felt a knowing inside me that there was something more and this led me from a path in black-and-white technical studies (electronic engineering) into the more subjective study of psychology, sociology and philosophy in my early twenties. I think if I had remained on this path, my true spiritual journey would have started there. I felt a calling to serve others at that time in my life that had been growing since I was a child, but I did not identify it with spirituality. My path took a turn when I met my now wife at university whilst studying applied social studies and we created our first son. I left university and went back to work in the electronics industry where I knew I could earn a reasonable wage and support my family. We have now been together for thirty years, we have two sons, one grandson and another grandchild on the way.

It wasn't until I was in my mid-forties and hit by a marital crisis and a pending breakup that I really started to do my inner work. A voyage of discovery that led me to re-examine my beliefs and my childhood experiences. I started to acknowledge the trauma that had existed in my life for the first time, having believed that I had an 'ideal' upbringing. I spoke for the first time to my wife and to our counsellor about what I now acknowledge as childhood sex abuse from a family member. I recognised my abandonment issues due to a father who was in the navy and was rarely home for the first five years of my life. I recognised my mum's emotionally and physically detached parenting, which I also recognise was developed from her childhood suffering and ongoing generational trauma. I acknowledged the emotional, physical and verbal abuse and bullying that I had received from my siblings. I experienced some dark times during that phase of my life but I now see it as an essential part of my growth.

I feel I needed to go to that challenging place in order to start the work of my soul awakening. I continue to work to recognise, heal and integrate the parts of my shadow self and I believe this is probably a lifetime's work for me and this work is closely paralleled by my spiritual development

My spiritual beliefs have guided me through trauma recovery and away from unhealthy conditioned patterns. Healing and shadow work have been key to my growth; for me, it has been about peeling back the layers of the conditioned self and the egoic self to find my true nature, which also includes discovering my true purpose for my time being in this body. I have spent a lot of time looking after the needs of my family as my children have grown up, but now as my second son has just left home, I feel I am able to follow my path and my destiny in pursuit of understanding my true nature, my life purpose and my spiritual self (my soul nature).

As I work to strip away the layers of conditioning and undoing, I feel I am finding my way back to myself. I can relate to the spiritual teachings of all religions and recognise the wisdom in those teachings, which I believe have in some cases been obscured and manipulate to serve the shadow aspects of individuals, groups and our present-day Western society and culture.

This process of recovery has been closely linked with my spiritual development, which has led me to listen many spiritual and religious books. Some of my favourite authors being Philip Shepherd, Reginald A Ray, Caroline Myss, David Deida, Osho, Eckhart Tolle, Ram Dass, Byron Katie and Tich Nhat Hanh. As well as a lot of reading I signed up for a six-month mentorship: the 'Priest of Phallic Power' is a closed men's group working to develop spirituality, healthy masculine sexuality, self-discovery and purpose. The development practices involved elements from shamanic, tantric, embodiment and meditative practices. This work has led me to recognise the struggles that many men are enduring in our society, which are resulting in unprecedentedly high levels of dysfunction, addiction, depression, anxiety and suicide. My primary purpose is to support men (and women) in their healing process.

I currently run a men's group, the 'Solent Men's Circle' and volunteer as a facilitator for 'Mentell', which provides online men's circles, both on a weekly basis.

Whilst these activities are not necessarily spiritually biased, it is my spiritual beliefs that support me in this work.

I also meditate, typically five days a week, and it is during these times that I feel my regular connection to the universe, to god, to source or whichever term you prefer to use. To me, all these terms are one and the same. I also feel deep connection to the universe at many other times, especially when in nature (I walk our dog twice a day in the South Downs), when working with likeminded groups and within my sexuality. I have also read many books on tantra and use some techniques on a regular basis to become a better lover, enhance my own sexual pleasure and ultimately to feel more connected with my partner and with the universe.

Today I still have some challenges around speaking my authentic truth in relation to my spiritual beliefs with my wider family and friends due to some fear of how I will be perceived. Fortunately, my wife is also on a similar journey, so we do have a deep mutual understanding and connection, and we are able to have open discussions without judgments. I am currently opening to the next stage of my learning that will be related to embodiment practices, practices for authentic connection (such as circling, authentic relating and surrendered leadership) breathwork and maybe experiments with psychedelics. I plan to bring this work to a wider audience through groupwork, retreats and online media.

My plan is that within the next five or six years, I will be able to consider retiring from my day job so that I can be 100 per cent focused and committed to my journey and to supporting others on theirs

4.5 Change the way you think: declutter, stretch, learn

In this section, we explore ways to expand our understanding and knowledge, and stretch ourselves out of our comfort zones. Sue describes her spiritual journey and shares how she left the relative safety of the corporate world to retrain, expand her awareness and start to give back to others in a way that was more aligned with her own sense of purpose.

4.5.1 Attend retreats and events that resonate

On the theme of following your highest excitement, go 'Google crazy' looking for retreats and get yourself on those that appeal and that you feel might stretch you. The energy of the group, and the boundless synchronous possibilities created by such events, is purely amazing. I think of them as the universe's 'open season' to connect yourself with complete strangers who can bring something amazing into your life, and you into theirs. And even if this particular aspect doesn't seem immediately apparent, the energy of the group will undoubtedly raise your vibration and, if you are open to it, set off a series of conscious and unconscious enquiries that will be about resonance and alignment and purpose and objectives in life.

4.5.2 Attend courses (including online) that appeal and that will raise your spiritual knowledge bank

For some time now, and especially since mid 2020, there has been a myriad of online courses available. Over the years I have attended courses from Robbins Maddanes Training, Mind Valley and Jack Canfield, amongst others. There is a vast range in price and they also come with differing degrees of interactions with the tutors and fellow students. It is certainly important to raise your spiritual knowledge by attending such events, as well as having fun with other likeminded people in a learning environment. Face-to-face is probably more desirable, but I have seen that virtual courses, even with large groups, can be effective. As there is so much on offer, it is important to follow what resonates with you, and perhaps give it a couple of days to sit with you before making a decision. Meditate and journal all aspects of taking up the course, and see where the process lands. It may be that you will come out with a resounding yes, I should join, or perhaps something even better will appear.

4.5.3 Do things that appeal but scare you—stretch your comfort zone and consciousness

As you focus on meditating and becoming more open to what might come your way, you may be offered opportunities and experiences that you would not normally consider. I think it is important to be open to exploring these fully. Obviously, a risk to life (yours and others) is to be avoided, but if these possibilities appear to push you out of your comfort zone and your only resistance is your fear, then it is useful to sit with these opportunities for a while. Try to explore where your fear and resistance is coming from, and what values they serve. It may be the outcome is that you are truly not interested in exploring the opportunity, or it might be that the resistance is a blockage that you need to work through in some way. Remember that fear and resistance can be complex and may represent a hidden issue, but they , like everything, arise for a reason. Be open and bold and face them head on, because by doing this you create the opportunity to grow and move forward on your path. Consider seeking help with the unblocking, for example through life coaches, NLP practitioners, energy healers, regression therapists and the myriad of other practitioners who work with unblocking historical limiting beliefs.

4.5.4 Explore different ways of approaching everything

In chapter three we explored the idea of living inside and outside of the Matrix. My proposition was that our three-dimensional world is a construct within which we 'do' our human living, but that we also have the ability to consciously experience our lives from a distance, that is, from outside of the Matrix. At the most basic level this involves constantly asking yourself questions such as 'why is this happening right now, to me'. This is not from the perspective of a victim, but from a position of understanding that everything happens for a reason and is an opportunity to align and live your purpose and grow. I constantly try to live my life in this way, in particular when I feel stress and fear. For example, a short while ago , in early January, I was on the London Orbital Motorway in the UK (the M25), on the way back from dropping my daughter at university for the start of the spring term. About forty minutes into the journey, the engine warning light lit on my dashboard and the temperature gauge hit red. I pulled over onto the hard shoulder straightaway and got out to make preparations to manage this situation. A short while after I arrived, a woman pulled over on the hard shoulder, just behind me. She was taking her teenage daughter back to school, had been losing power in her car, and had stopped and get help. Unfortunately, she had parked closely behind my car, which was still billowing smoke or steam from the engine and, as I thought, was at risk of blowing up. This led to an interesting set of interactions as I tried to get her to reverse away from my car, which she struggled to do, at times getting very close to the fast moving traffic on the carriageway. I found myself experiencing a mix of emotions—from concern, to dread, to a sense of responsibility for the safety of her and her daughter, and a degree of disbelief that she didn't understand the scale of the danger that the three of us were in so close to a fast moving 4 lane motorway. Over the next three hours 'in the Matrix', she was rescued, I had to handle delays and poor communication from my rescue company while my phone and car batteries slowly died and I got increasingly cold from being outside away from my car and walking up and down behind the safety barrier to try to keep warm in the January cold. Eventually, I was picked up and transported home, along with my car. Outside the Matrix', when not focused on my personal needs, I was considering what was going on, and why? What was the growth opportunity for me here? What was I to learn from this and the various interactions associated with this episode? Was she the angel sent to keep me company, or was I the angel sent to keep her company and give her reassurance? Or was this an issue about my vigilance of the car prior to driving, the learning moment for me? A few days later, it transpired that the radiator had cracked due to age, a not uncommon issue with this particular model after fifteen years, so this could not have been avoided—but maybe there were opportunities to manage its impact better?

So although it can at times be a 'strain on the brain' to constantly drop inside and outside of what is going on, to ask constantly why things are happening, I feel it can help to reduce the stress of situations and obviously support growth as you reflect on your own reactions to situations as they occur real time, instead of a while later.

It is possible that this level of real-time reflection might help you make better decisions. For instance, it may stop you from making an immediate reaction to an event, which you might regret in hindsight. Verbal fights or text/email battles are a great example of this. Even if you write the 'killer blow' response, which may help to discharge all the tension and anger you are feeling at the time, it may be a better idea to delete it and step outside of the situation for long enough to reflect on what is going on, and why you are feel and responding in the way that you are. This can be a powerful way to reduce stress, grow and probably resolve the conflict in a shorter, more effective way.

It is important to remember that everything is a choice. Everything. We are familiar with the phrase 'he/she made me feel that way, and so made me do that'. This is common with children of course, but for many it extends well into adulthood. Although we may find this hard to accept, life is only about our reaction to events and situations. Everything is essentially neutral. What makes life, you could argue, is the colour, flavour and texture of our responses to them.

Sue's Story

Describe your spirituality

I'm still on the journey of re-membering myself home. What do I mean by that? I mean that I still need to keep reminding myself to reconnect over and over again to that which isn't visible, isn't tangible, but can be deeply felt and experienced; the universal energy that is always flowing through me. A sense of connection, being truly present within myself and to the energy around me that feels like I'm coming home to a deep truth and re-membering myself, re-uniting myself with it and becoming a member again of something timeless, universal and energetic.

And then there's reality! I can still easily get caught up in the day-to-day material world and forget that at my core, my essence, my soul, I am not my flesh, bones, thoughts, emotions. And yet, whenever I relax my body and mind, and tune in, I re-member that I Am. I Am vibration, energy, spirit—wave, not particle. Essentially energy and not matter.

I'll likely never know if any of this is 'true' and I'm okay with that. It's a perspective that helps me feel my way through life, especially when events and situations seem challenging. And I find it comforting to believe that there's something to experience beyond this corporeal body's life experience and that energy doesn't die when the body dies, but that it morphs, changes, transmutes, transports to another plane and another kind of experience.

Spirituality for me is a way to make sense of some of life's experiences, to sense and connect to the energetic field around us, and to feel part of something beyond me. It's like a comfort blanket for my body, mind and soul and a way to re-member myself home!

What is your earliest memory of spiritual awakening?

I remember going to church as a brownie guide, around age seven. It was a very strange affair and I never felt at home. I guess at this early stage of life I already had an unrecognised sense that there was something 'larger than me' but it didn't seem to fit with this religious faith approach that I was experiencing through church, and I hadn't yet gained a sense of it for myself or the language to try and explain any of it.

How did you feel? What challenges did you face?

I finally began to believe in something 'other than' this physical plane when I was fourteen and in an amateur dramatics play. My mum was helping backstage and one of the cast told her that she'd been here before. That got me thinking about the idea of reincarnation and ghosts, spirits and life after death, or life during death, or death during life, and wondering what all these different states were about.

In my early twenties I had some very strange experiences, for example, where a strong metal corkscrew with two arms suddenly became a metal corkscrew with one arm—the other literally sheared off overnight in my living room. And a pencil that dropped from the sky between a colleague and I. And lifts and lights that started going on and off on their own when I was around.

This mostly then stopped until my mid-thirties, when I met a couple who were reiki masters, and with whom I had some of my first more obvious energy experiences. I began to sense them changing the energy in the room, and I witnessed them almost invisibly move through crowds or create space around them seemingly by doing nothing. It piqued my curiosity again about the layers of invisible forces that we live in and with, and how they can be utilised, or interacted with.

It made me feel somewhat inadequate that I didn't understand how to interact with this unknown force for myself, and in awe of those that did. It felt completely surreal and yet at the same time almost more real than anything tangible like the tables and chairs in a room. I remember thinking how much my mum would probably 'get' that I was curious about these experiences and yet also thinking that the rest of my family would likely dismiss it as nonsense, and think that I was 'off with the fairies' or 'in la-la-land!'

My real challenges with a more spiritually aware life didn't come until I was in Sydney.

What happened next?

I lived in Sydney for five years and this is where my spiritual awakening really began. I experienced really strong reiki from someone while I was having a coughing fit: it stopped instantly as I felt the force of energy coming into my body. I experienced massive shifts through crystal healings, sound therapy, just being in a room with spiritually awakened people, acupuncture, oneness ceremonies, huna work. All sorts of things that were mainstream and easily accessible in Sydney that I'd not even heard of in the UK at that time.

I had my first experience of consciously expanding and contracting my own energy, my first experience of meditation, and many experiences of feeling like the new kid on the block around people who had way more spiritual understanding than I.

I met people who channelled, psychics, people who

could see auras, people who found energy vortices and did dowsing. All sorts of ways to connect with the invisible web that holds everything together. And I loved it. I often felt a bit on the outside because I was very much in discovery mode. I couldn't 'do it', or explain it properly, or understand any of it fully. But I was welcomed into a spiritual land. There was an ancient quality of the land and the sense of 'Dreamtime' and tribal ancestry that felt very different from the energy of the UK. And I was able to explore spirituality in a very expansive way over there.

A key moment?

There were actually two. The first was experiencing a oneness ceremony in a room of about 2,000 people during a Tony Robbins 'Date with Destiny' event. The energy in the room was intense and I felt wave after wave coursing through me, unlike anything I'd ever experienced before. I now interpret this as a strong chakra alignment, a strong connection to universal energy, and brainwaves that had potentially tipped into gamma waves for a short while, creating a kind of bliss state. But at the time I had no idea what was going on, except that it felt incredible, I had tears of joy and gratitude, and I wanted it to last forever. When meditating I can sometimes re-connect to that feeling, but it's never as strong as being in a room with 2,000 others also focusing on oneness. That experience convinced me more than ever that I was able to connect into and become part of the universal energetic field.

The second key experience was about a year before

leaving Sydney to come back to the UK. I was running a course in my home and two of the participants said that they'd seen the same spirit in the room. At the end of the course one of the participants who'd had a sighting taught me a cleansing process. I said that I was only renting the house and that if the spirit lived here and I was transient then it didn't feel ecological to try and clear her from her own space. But it was explained to me that she belonged to a different timeline and was trapped here. And the process was about making peace with the spirits in the house, so that they had an invitation and a way to leave if they wanted to. But that I wouldn't be forcing anything.

I discussed it with my husband, and we decided to go through with it. Because I spent more time in the home than he did, I did the ceremony part. We both noticed a massive difference when we returned to the house twenty-four hours later. The energy in the house somehow felt flat. Neutral. Neither of us had sensed the spirit before, but there was a noticeable shift on our return, and we agreed to focus on playing happy music, filling the space with love and laughter to create new positive energy for the home.

This absolutely cemented my belief that there are ways of being other than in this physical realm that we're living in, although to this day I'm still open-minded about whether it's life after death or trapped spirits or parallel universes.

During those years in Sydney my inner hippie was definitely released, and I felt more at home in so many ways than I've ever felt in the UK. Being spiritual was acceptable, welcomed, embraced by so many open-minded and open-hearted people. I am deeply grateful for that time and feel that this was truly the start of my spiritual journey.

The challenges of becoming more spiritually aware and open

My time in Australia was when I also left mainstream employment and delved into the world of personal development as a self-employed trainer, facilitator and coach. My eyes started to open to the power of the mind, perception, beliefs and manifestation as well as all the energy and spiritual experiences. I began to learn about life through the lens of some of the universal laws and the level of self-responsibility for creating/co-creating every result in my life. The movie *The Secret* came out and interest in the law of attraction and the manifestation of material things exploded.

In many ways learning about all of the personal development stuff was ground-breaking and empowering. And in many ways it rocked my previous life tenets to the core, so that it was a bit like the start of a very long dark night of the soul. Suddenly I was supposed to be limitless and yet everywhere I looked I saw limitation. I was supposed to be abundant and yet everywhere I looked I realised how impoverished and scarcity mindset I was. The veil had been lifted, and in truth I didn't much like what I saw. And I was supposed to be able to use all my newfound tools and techniques to effectively 'heal' myself. But in truth, I felt torn apart in so many ways. What I'd believed was true, no longer was. To use the Matrix analogy I'd taken the red pill and now I couldn't get back to the blue pill land I used to know. I yearned to be like Neo. And yet I continued to feel discontented, unable to reach my potential, frustrated, lacking in belief in myself, in my life, in the world. I now knew I co-created my reality—but I didn't yet have the spiritual, mental, emotional fortitude, understanding, or experience to get life back on track. And so a slow, insidious descent lasting many years occurred.

Through all of this time I had moments of re-membering, of coming back home to what feels most true, and feeling the comfort and strength of being supported by the universe and being a spiritual being. But then I'd get pulled and caught back into three-dimensional material world of worries, or events.

So, after leaving Australia and the support network of spiritual people, my growth stagnated for a while. It's only really been in the past few years, that I've started to solidify any sense of continued spiritual connection.

I've been lucky enough to have some connection with some wonderful women in the UK, who are more awakened spiritually, and I've discovered new teachers and guides, like Dr Joe Dispenza, whose meditations are a constant source of joy and peace to me. I've also been deepening my understanding of energy and meditation through being a member of Mind Valley, Neurogym and taking part in UK-based in-person workshops.

As I've begun to build out this spiritual re-membering and reconnection, so my faith in myself and the universal source energy has started to deepen.

What does your spiritual day/week look like now?

I aim to meditate daily. Ideally this will be for thirty to sixty minutes soon after waking up, although sometimes it happens before I go to bed

I aim to be mindful during the day, tuning into the present moment, quietening my mind, closing my eyes and expanding my awareness for a couple of minutes here and there.

I also love going for a walk most days and, when I'm not in a hurry, I enjoy drinking in the natural sight: the radiance of a flower or some berries, the way the light is shining through the trees and casting shadows on the grass, the sound of the birds or hugging a tree and feeling its energy interacting with mine. If I'm not able to go for a walk, then I like to dance 5Rhythms, stretch, do some resistance training or go for a swim. I always feel more alive and spiritually connected when there's some way to move my body and be active each day.

I really notice a difference in my resilience, groundedness and creativity on the days that I do vs don't meditate and move my body.

And of course, then there's gratitude. The cornerstone of it all. How grateful I am to feel supported every day. Even when my outside world has been crumbling, there has been a growing sense of inner faith and gratitude, which is strengthened every time I remember to connect in and be part of the universal energy field.

How do you feel now?

I still miss the accessibility and acceptability of spirituality and all things energy-related that I experienced in Sydney, although spirituality and energy are much more widely accepted in the UK now than they were in the early 2000s.

I am deeply grateful to one of my two deeply spiritual friends from Sydney whom I now speak with regularly. Her perspective and connection are deeply grounding to be around and I'm always inspired and uplifted by my connection with her.

I feel glad to have the ability to connect energetically. At some point I will take time to explore the energy side of things more fully and learn something like reiki. Ultimately, I would like to be a clear enough channel and have enough awareness and skill to be able to support remote healings.

My current perspective on life is that we are all energetic beings having a physical experience, and that our energy will transmute into a different form at our physical death. I am intrigued by the quantum energy perspective of being able to collapse space and time and draw experiences to you rather than working to 'make' things happen in the physical world. However, I am still a beginner on this path.

I am willing to hold all of my current beliefs about spirituality from the perspective of having a beginner's mind: not needing to know the answers, and being willing to upgrade or change my answers as new insights, experiences and awareness awakens within me.

I believe that life/the universe has my back. And that things are happening for me and not against me. I believe that if I act positively, kindly and in alignment with myself then good things will unfold.

What have you learned about your practical spirituality and the human experience

I've learned a lot about how much smoother and calmer I feel on the days where I do take time for some meditation, mindful movement, or connected creativity and those days where they get sidelined.

I've also learned that some key beliefs help me to travel through life with a little more equanimity and calm than I used to. They may sound trite because you've probably heard them reeled off at various personal development trainings or spiritual events. But I find them comforting and nourishing. They are:

- Everything's unfolding as it should
- I made a contract to come here to evolve in some way. And when I feel like I'm off track, lost, uncertain, I can have faith that I'm on a co-created journey and even if I choose to go down some blind alleys,it's inevitable that I'll re-discover the more resonant path (the one I contracted to be on) over time.
- I believe that I'm here to learn and help others to learn certain spiritual lessons and that this will all happen somehow through the course of my life. When I stop learning I'll die.
- I am safe. I am whole. I am perfect. I am imperfect. I am growing. All of these are great in theory and a lot harder to remember in the reality of every day. And when I forget them, or stuff things up and feel a bit sorry for myself, I'm learning how valuable it is to have self-compassion and I remind myself that I am human, and that's okay!
- There is abundance and I am worthy of enjoying that

experience in all aspects of my life. This is definitely still a major work in progress for me.

To me spirituality is about expansiveness, unboundedness, and the ability to create, explore and express. It's about working with what is, and what can be, and not being constrained by, or limited by, conventional rules.

And that is why the universal energy approach and spirituality is more aligned to my way of being than any religion could be. Although energetic vibration and waveform can be measured and documented, that doesn't define them, because they are constantly in motion and changing.

Universal energy and spirituality is available to everyone and anyone. It is egalitarian and that is something that I value deeply.

4.6 Consciously manage your state: learn to be present, improve your dreaming and explore altered states

In this section we explore the idea of being present, the power of dreaming and journeys into altered states. Sharon shares her experience of her spirituality and how presence and a conscious connection with All That Is frames her human experience now and supports her giving back to others.

4.6.1 Being present

Being present could be considered an extension of the idea that there is only now. One true moment. No past or future. Just now. Thus, to connect with your human experience, you benefit from connecting at all levels with the present. As part of their research into the Japanese idea of ikigai, Héctor García and Francesc Miralles describe takumis—artisans who dedicate their lives to a single activity, with a focus on perfection that is close to an obsession (Garcia & Miralles, 2017). They are said to be continually in the moment with their work and art. The ancient art of the Japanese tea ceremony, said to have been influenced by Zen Buddhist monks, and ikebana (Japanese flower arranging) are practices that require the participant to be present with the practice, to be at one with it on every level of their being.

Being present can be improved through practice, like most things in life. The idea is that to practise being present, you need to focus on one single thing. Be aware of every aspect of that one thing and how your body, sensations and thoughts are reacting and responding. Don't be too bothered about the actions of your mind as it struggles to settle. Don't try to fight the thoughts it generates. Just calmly acknowledge them and let them go, with love, and come back to your focus. You will probably have to do this many times. Taking a break from time to time is fine. As you continue your practice, you should begin to notice how concerns and worries become less important and a sense of enjoyment in your focus and task takes over. It is important to be grateful and have joy for every step, every tactile sensation and aspect of our task.

A great example of being present is drinking tea. In the words of the Buddhist monk Thich Nhat Hanh: 'Drink your tea slowly and reverently, as if it were the axis on which the earth revolves—slowly, evenly, without rushing toward the future. Live the actual moment. Only this moment is life.' Another great quote from Thich is, 'Walk as if you are kissing the earth with your feet.' When you practise walking meditation, this is the kind of visualisation you can use to feel grounded and connected and present with the practice and the surroundings and your body. It is a great way to train yourself in being present.

This process of deep focus, especially on a simple task, changes your perspective and paradigm, and raises your vibration, because it connects you with interaction and joy on a higher energetic level. Through this interaction you have the opportunity to have an amazing experience from the most simplest of activities. If you look back in your past you may be able to remember moments when you were definitely present, or 'in the zone'. In her story, Suzanne describes how she discovered the fantastic experience of being present when she took up painting in her fifties.

4.6.2 Improve your dreaming

What is dreaming? There is a multitude of written material out there on this question, from shamanism, mysticism, spirituality, history and science. It would be an injustice to the myriad practitioners, authors and researchers involved in the subject to try and summarise it here. If you recall what I said in chapter three, you will know that I believe that when we dream, we shut down our three-dimensional bodies and return to our spiritual and normal states. In fact, when our human body goes to sleep, our true state—spirit—wakes up. Our spirit never actually goes to sleep, but shutting down our bodies for a few hours allows a greater connection between our human three-dimensional selves and our subconscious spiritual beings.

Since the first humans walked on Earth, our species has dreamed, as have all mammalian organisms. In Stephen Larsen and Tom Verner's book on the subject, *The Transformational Power of Dreaming*, they point out that for some, dreaming can be a lucid, detailed, specific and sometimes controlled experience, for example shamans; for others, it feels like sporadic memories, random incoherent images and short stories; and some are not conscious of dreaming at all.

So, dreaming provides access to a different realm of consciousness. In dreams we seem to arrive in a situation, without knowing how we got there: it's like the curtain goes up on a play and no backstory has yet been given. This strange experience is captured by the film *Inception* (Nolan, 2010). In one scene, the main protagonist, Cob, played by Leonardo DiCaprio, asks his young protégé Ariadne, played by Elliot Page, how they got here, to which they have no answer—until they realise they are in a dream.

4.6.3 Creating altered states of consciousness

In section 4.1 we explored the importance of meditation in breaking down the barriers and blockages between our three-dimensional selves and higher consciousness, in order to reduce the 'mind clutter' of our physical world and consciously realign with higher consciousness and life purposes. In doing this, we are going some way towards creating an altered state.

An altered state of consciousness is a temporary change in one's normal mental state without being considered unconscious. These states can be created intentionally, or they can happen by accident, or due to illness. People intentionally try to attain an altered state for various motives, including religious and spiritual reasons, to relax, or to improve their physical and mental health, where hypnosis can be effective. Involuntary altered states can occur during high fevers, when we can have convincing hallucinations. They can also be caused by dreaming or daydreaming, the process of childbirth, and during sleep deprivation, sexual euphoria, or panic.

Altered states of consciousness have been used by humans for more than 30,000 years. According to the *Wiley–Blackwell Handbook of Transpersonal Psychology*, excessive dancing, meditation and mind-altering plants were used in ancient civilizations to modulate the activity of the mind. The neuroscientist Anne-Laure Le Cunff, in her book *Altered States of Consciousness: The Elusiveness of the Mind*, suggests there are many forms of non-ordinary mental states, all of which seem to distort our sense of space and time.

She writes: 'In extraordinary states of consciousness—moments of shock, meditation, sudden mystical experiences, near-death experiences, under the influence of drugs—temporal consciousness is fundamentally altered. Hand-in-hand with this goes an altered consciousness of space and self. In these extreme circumstances, time and concepts of space and self are modulated together—intensified or weakened together. But in more ordinary situations, too, such as boredom, the experience of flow, and idleness, time and self are collectively altered.' (Wittmann, 2018)

The five altered states of consciousness

According to Le Cunff, ways of inducing altered states of consciousness include breathwork, dance, lucid dreaming, sexual intercourse, sleep deprivation, fasting, music, meditation, sensory deprivation, hypnosis, psychoactive substances and physical exercise. In 2012, Dieter Vaitl of the Bender Institute of Neuroimaging in Germany proposed a model with five distinct altered states of consciousness. These are:

Pharmacological

(Including plant medicines such as ayahuasca and hapé)

This category covers short-term changes in the general configuration of one's individual experiences caused by psychoactive substances. Many of these work by shifting levels of neurotransmitters in the brain, causing changes in awareness and behaviour.

Psychological

(Including meditation, hypnotherapy, past-life regression, ecstatic dance, shamanic drumming, singing and energy healing techniques such as reiki)

Hypnosis can lead to reduced peripheral awareness as well as an enhanced capacity to respond to suggestion, and music therapy can increase relaxation and decrease anxiety.

Reiki energy healing is about accessing universal life force energy to activate and support the body's natural ability to heal. Often during reiki healing and training, participants experience energy flows, lights, sensations and colours as the energy flows through and around the body. I am a reiki practitioner, and after one session a client described leaving her body. I have also witnessed this during my reiki training. These experiences are the creation of altered states as vibration increases and consciousness shifts to allow apparently extraordinary events to occur.

Physical and physiological

(Including lucid dreaming, astral dreaming projection, trance journeying, dream journeys, tantric sex)

Humanity's use of dream states and dream journeys extends at least 65,000 years, and quite possibly much longer than that, if the Australian first nation people were typical. Dream journeying and connection with an alternative spiritual world within the dream state is an embedded aspect of their way of life. Most ancient peoples on Earth have knowledge and experience and connection with other realities through the dream state. Traditionally, shamans used this ability to support their people through protection and healing. Shamans are alive and well today, and practising across the planet and growing in numbers, particularly in parts of the world, such as Western Europe and North America, where religious and science-based attitudes led to their public demise over the past few hundred years.

Guidance on how to access the dream state and control dream journeys is prolific, as is guidance on techniques. A non-exhaustive list includes: *Astral Projection for Beginners* (McCoy, 1999), *Trance Journeys of the Hunter Gatherers* (Brink, 2016), *Wise Women of the Dreamtime* (Parker & Lambert, 1993) and *The Transformational Power of Dreaming* (Larsen & Verner, 2017).

Another path to altered states in this category is tantric sex. This is a component of tantra, an ancient approach to life mentioned in the Vedas, which, as we learned earlier in this chapter, were written more than 4,000 years ago.

Tantra involves several practices, including yoga and mantras as well as sexual intercourse. These texts and rituals are found in more esoteric forms of Buddhism and Hinduism, and sex is just one form of tantra, which is part of a tradition practised by a small number of people. In general terms, tantric sex is performed to achieve a kind of ecstasy or enlightenment, because tantra is at its core a spiritual practice. For Hindu practitioners, that means working with a guru to achieve 'liberation' through tantric sex, and; for Buddhist practitioners, the goal is enlightenment. Sometimes, tantric yoga is a component. Sometimes, tantra is practised without literal sex at all. In this case, the people engaging in the act avoid doing it for purely pleasure-seeking motives—in Buddhism, this is believed to have undesirable karmic consequences. As a whole, it's important to note that tantra, in its traditional forms, may include sex, but it isn't concerned with sexual connection or even greater intimacy—and especially not with having your best orgasm ever.

However, like any Eastern practice that's been adopted (or possible appropriated), the journey from its origin has passed through a myriad of sometimes cloudy interpretations over many years, which means that the common understanding in many parts of the world, and particularly the West, is that tantra equals amazing sex and multiple orgasms. This might be considered by some as 'neo-tantra', the form that developed in the West in the twentieth century, and which somewhat divorces the practice from its spiritual roots in favour of a sexually focused alternative.

Closer to the mark is the common understanding that tantric sex may be defined as a slow, meditative form of intercourse where the end goal is not orgasm so much as enjoying the sexual journey and its sensations, with the aim of moving sexual energy through the body for healing, transformation and enlightenment. One partner may give the other a slow, full-body massage to learn about their body and help awaken their sexual energy. This may also help a person become in tune with their partner's wants and desires.

Also consistent with ancient knowledge is the modern understanding that breathing is an integral part of tantric sex. This is partly because it revolves around meditation, which can use similar breathing exercises, such as breathing deeply from the diaphragm. When engaging in tantric sex with a partner, synchronising the breath may increase connection and intimacy. So tantric sex is a meditative sexual practice that encourages people to focus on mind–body connections. This can lead to fulfilling sexual experiences and greater intimacy.

With specific reference to the female sexual orgasm, it is suggested in the journal 'Socioaffective Neuroscience and Psychology' (Safron, 2016, Vol 6.1), that 'the experience of orgasm can be explained as an 'intensification of sexual pleasure' and a deepening of 'altered states of consciousness'. The author argues 'that sexual activity can lead to increased focus, which reduces our conscious thinking and allows us to become absorbed in the sensory experience. This is a trance-like state, an experience that also occurs during meditation, when the mind is focused on the breath, candlelight or other object. You can, of course, enter a trance state by yourself, while meditating, painting, washing dishes or exercising. But when you are with a sexual partner, your nervous systems synchronises not only with the rhythmic activity of sex, but also with each other. This increases your sense of connection with your partner, and weakens the boundaries between self and other as the me–you duality fades away.'

Other research was carried out by H Umit Sayin, an academic at Istanbul University, and published as 'Altered States of Consciousness Occurring During Expanded Sexual Response in the Human Female (Neuro quantology, 2011). This provides an extensive list of subjective feelings and altered states of consciousness experience by the women involved in a study, as illustrated by this passage:

'Expanded sexual response (ESR) is a recently defined phenomenon. It is defined as 'being able to attain long lasting, prolonged, multiple and/or sustained orgasms that were longer and more intense than the classical orgasm patterns defined in the literature'.

'During our detailed preliminary survey to investigate the claimed ESR phenomenon in some particular women, we also investigated subjective feelings and altered states of consciousness (ASC) during intense and prolonged orgasms in women experiencing ESR. During our preliminary survey, seventy-two types of subjective feelings and ASC patterns were described in the forty-seven women with ESR. Among these were: depersonalisation; out of body experience; flying; a feeling of dying (*petite mort*); ecstasy; rapture; explosive feelings; quivering, earthquake feelings; flooding; absorbing; spurting; blessed; shuddering; intense love; unreal; surreal; voyage to nature; seeing flashes of light and colour, geometric shapes, figures; peacefulness; physical and spiritual warmth; loss of control; spreading; flowing; mystical experience; unification with the partner and/or the universe; déjà vu; crying.

'It is concluded that in some women with ESR, the intense and prolonged orgasms induce a form of ASC whose mechanism is not explained yet. Pudental, pelvic, hypogastric and vagus nerves, as well as oxytocin pathways, are involved in the development of female orgasm. We hypothesise that blended activation among these four nerves during ESR may be inducing extraordinary subjective feelings and ASC during profound female orgasms. The "four-nerve theory of female orgasm" may explain the ASC during ESR to some extent. Also, involvement of dopaminergic, serotoninergic, noradrenergic, opioid, prolactinergic and oxytocinergic pathways may modulate the altered mood states during ESR-induced ASCs.'

According to Richard Asimus (a leading tantric teacher),

tantra was created by yogic masters to learn how to shatter the preoccupation with the ego that is at the root of every person's body, in the primal root of sexual energy. He suggests that by acquiring tools to shift energetic vigour, whether through breathing, meditation, or other activities, consciousness may be shifted. He describes tantra as 'literally meaning "to expand, manifest or interweave". It is a practice of staying in the moment and being completely aware and present at all times. It is a practice of allowing the sexual energy to bring us to an altered state of consciousness. It is a mutual journey and adventure that extends arousal, creating psychological and energetic changes.'

You can find out more by researching tantra and tantric sex, including the work of Richard Asimus, as well as Patricia Johnson and Mark Michaels, authors of *The Essence of Tantric Sexuality* (Michaels & Johnson, 2006) and the facilitators of tantric seminars. They suggest, speaking about the many tantric meditations that promote truly loving oneself, that 'the vast majority of tantra practices are not sexual and most of them are done alone. You must know the divine in yourself before you are able to find it with others'.

Pathological

(Including out-of-body and near-death experiences)
This book is not suggesting that we should go out and try to create this kind of state; I simply note, for the sake of completeness, that out-of-body and near-death experiences are real. The latter can follow traumatic events, and survivors often report being aware of leaving their body and going on a journey that involves a tunnel and light, and facing a choice between returning to their earth-bound life or moving on to

the next stage of existence. This experience often leads to a fundamental change in their approach to life and a renewed sense of purpose, usually associated with a greater sense of compassion.

Conventional medicine suggests that this may happen because such an experience fundamentally changes the way the brain works. Is it possible that a traumatic experience causing brain damage can lead to an altered state of consciousness? According to Jeffrey Avner (Avner, 2006), patients report either reduced self-awareness and increased overall awareness, or an increased awareness of the environment.

Spontaneous

(Including increased awareness of spiritual experiences and growth, and daydreaming)

Altered states can occur when our minds wander. Like dreaming, daydreaming can involve images, memories and feelings that feel real, as well as the reactions that go with them. Several studies have shown that daydreaming may be the brain's default setting when we're not actively engaged in a task, and that the default mode network, which is associated with this default setting, is more active when we are daydreaming. Should daydreaming then be considered a normal state of consciousness, rather than an altered state?

Maybe instead of considering a default state and a myriad of altered states, we need to contemplate the possibility that all states of consciousness are all equally important modes of perception. Some may seem more useful to functioning productively in our world—making decisions, navigating our immediate environment, communicating with those around us—but none is more valid than the others.

Any mental state forms an elusive part of consciousness as a whole (Le Cunff, 2022).

Sharon's story

Spirituality leading to pure love

I wouldn't describe myself as a 'spiritual' person. To me, the term feels like a label that doesn't fit. I am life, I am source energy and I am pure love. After having experienced different stages of being, from consuming life to the question of who am I, from explorations into the past, discovering old traumas and letting go of them, from experiencing different forms of energy healing to the pure form of healing that doesn't need any tools or techniques I finally came home to what I always was and will be: Pure Love—the human experience minus trauma and programming.

My earliest stage of playing with the elements was at the age of nineteen, when the daughter of friends of our family died in a plane crash. She was buried and I found myself visiting her grave and asking her to give me a sign—when suddenly the wind would pick up as if she were answering through it. I repeated this many times and it was always the same response. Her mother was not able to let her go, so I felt that she was still around in some kind of odd way. Soon I went to England as an au pair and was introduced to some church event that turned out to be more of a seance than anything else. It freaked me out as I was sure that she might contact me right there in front of everyone and I felt a strong urge to just flee. After that experience I dropped the topic of experiencing the other world for quite a while and just went on with my life.

Later, when I was studying at university, I had some health issues that after long search was found to be chronic. Phases of not being well came in and out and by the time I started a family I would collect further chronic diseases. The classic medical treatments didn't make me feel any better, so I searched for alternatives like acupuncture and imaginative therapy. I was also healing family patterns that reached way back, with the help of the work of family constellations. The result was that I found a way to see the easily forgivable patterns at work within every human being. I looked for something that I could learn to assist others in finding their peace within. All of the techniques that I considered useful took years of practice and large sums of money, which I both wasn't willing to spend. I then stumbled upon a seminar in Reconnective Healing® which I—or better my body—responded to immediately. That was back in 2014.

I practised Reconnective Healing® regularly with a group of friends in Frankfurt to gain more and more confidence in my or its abilities. I entered the quantum roam and understood how frequency is key in managing everyday life. By this time my parents were worried that I had become a quack.

In 2016 I spent the summer in Washington, DC, with my two sons. They slept in so that gave me some me time to sit on the porch for hours in the mornings listening to Dr Steven Greer and his wisdom on anti-gravitational technologies and other inventions that humanity apparently just wasn't yet ready for. At that time I also had a spiritual teacher that made me see the I AM, so there I was in hot and humid DC fighting with cognitive dissonance and very shocked about life in the capital of the US.

So Reconnective Healing® taught me how to bring people back into alignment. But when they fell back onto their own two feet, that's when the actual work seemed to start: that's when one had to face the trauma, get rid of layers and layers of programming to finally experience one's true self and calling. In the process I practised killing my ego in only ninety-nine days, to the extent that my body came down with a severe case of vertigo. But this, too, passed.

Over time, my experience was that there was no need for a teacher or a technique, and that in the end life is quite simple: trust the universe and get out of your own way so that life can actually live itself. There is an innate intelligence at work that you shouldn't mess with. I trained that muscle and finally trusted that everything that enters my life served a purpose and every circumstance passed. Relaxing into that amazing intelligence and watching the beautiful order that lies at the bottom of ALL THAT IS gave me peace and calm. I became aware of the highly geometrical structure and the syntropy that orchestrates life on all planes.

Today I trust my path. I eat and cook what feels natural in the specific moment, I naturally do the work that comes my way with a lot of joy. I have new customers in my advertising job and every now and then I have clients that come for a session or for some coaching. In the end, the work in both areas comes down to the same: I see the human, I get a feeling of what is needed and wanted and what matches my fellow human on the path right now and I, or the other, receive a gift from the field of endless potential.

4.7 Think and reflect ... but make sure you TAKE ACTION

In this section we explore the importance and tools for self-reflection and the power of right positive thinking and affirmation, supported by action—the principles of the manifestation concept. Christina shares stories of her effective use of positive thought and actions to achieve tangible positive outcomes.

Throughout this book there is plenty of guidance on reflection, but it is also important to take action. Reflection is extremely important as a way to force yourself to stop, take a breath, let life's clutter pass on by and allow yourself to re-ground yourself and your environment, for instance through meditation (see section 4.1) and being in nature. Using these processes to reconnect with your higher self, realign with purpose and allow space for guidance and inspiration to become visible is important—and then, using this and your best sense of intuition and gut feeling, you need to take action.

Supported by the work of many renowned personal development coaches, such as Tony Robbins (Robbins, 1989) and Jack Canfield (Canfield & Switzer, 2005), I have concluded from years of exploring manifestation of desires, especially money and abundance, that you have to take action to create the environment for the universe to work its magic. Napoleon Hill, through his book *Think and Grow Rich* (Hill, 1937) is one of the earliest modern-day writers to take this approach. It is suggested that Hill may have drawn some inspiration from earlier works, included *The Science of Getting Rich* by the New Thought Movement writer Wallace D Wattles (Wattles, 1910). Just sitting at home wishing and waiting for your dreams and ambitions to come true will not work, even if you are using the most in-depth meditation techniques.

The idea of directed thought supported by action has been explored in increasing depth for millennia, and given particular focus in the late nineteenth century, ahead of Wattles and Hill, by many, including the New Thought Movement. It is suggested that *The Science of Getting Rich* is based on the Hindu philosophies that 'one is all, and all is one' (see the preface), and on what Wattles called 'the certain way of thinking'.

The universe appears to use your three-dimensional world of stuff and events and potential engagement and the 7.6 billion people you share the planet with to make things happen, through what may appear to be coincidences but are actually synchronicities. But we have to set our intent and really feel the outcome that we desire, thus creating the energetic vibration of having it. In this way the power of the universe matches this vibration, allowing the desire to appear in our reality.

The movie *The Secret,* based on the book of the same name (Byrne, 2006), explores this idea in some depth, that is, the Law of Attraction, which suggests that abundance comes from all aspects of life, not just money: for example, love, security, giving back, good health, contentment, adventure, connection with nature and many other aspects of our complex lives.

It is also suggested that having set our intent, and created the feeling of having it, we need to be detached from the outcome—which can be a real challenge. If you are coming from a place of perceived lack, and this is the message you send out to the universe, then it is suggested that the universe reacts by sending you more lack. So, you need to almost fool the universe by creating the feeling of already having it and feeling good about having it, perhaps by surrounding yourself with things and taking part in events that make you feel like you already have it.

An old family friend achieved this by test-driving expensive cars and buying *Forbes* magazine and similar symbols of wealth as part of his manifestation process of creating the feeling of having and being the financially abundant person he wanted to be. Today he is a millionaire and owns all of those items and the lifestyle he aspired to.

Therefore, we also need to make ourselves available and active to allow the universe do to its thing. For instance, if you are wishing for your dream home, then you need to have the right positive thinking, but also be taking action by searching estate agents' sites, visiting properties and talking to mortgage providers in a positive way. Show your positive intent by looking for your dream property, but also be aware and open to whatever may come along, however unusual and unaligned it may appear, at first, to be.

In this way, the energy of the universe can create situations where a series of events can occur that lead you to your dream, or something better. This is a critical point because the universe has the capacity to conceive of an infinite number of outcomes, in contrasts to our human capacity. So, it is possible that this process could result in you being offered an opportunity that actually exceeds your initial dream. Be open, be aware of what comes into your visibility. Use meditation to connect with the truth of the options presented and your true (non-mind) feelings about them. If they feel good and right, despite what your mind is saying, then they are worth exploring.

One caveat I would add to this is the question/comment 'if it is aligned with your purpose'. I believe that this is an underpinning requirement in achieving your goals and dreams, and one that on a universal and spiritual level will dictate what occurs. Many of us dream of winning the National Lottery but acquiring vast amounts of money comes with its own energy, challenges and opportunities to learn and grow, and that particular route for growth may not be the destiny or life-pathway for most of us.

From an energetic level, by taking action, we are saying to the universe that we are ready to align ourselves with our aspirations and our purpose, and in so doing our vibration also changes to align with those people, situations and items that will allow us to achieve them, and so they become visible to us. Even the smallest of actions create this vibration, so it's important to just start, as reflected in the words of Dr Martin Luther King, Jr: 'Take the first step in faith. You don't have to see the whole staircase, just the first step.'

4.7.1 Journal your life experience

I cannot overstate the importance and usefulness of journaling for me. On the most basic level, it helps me to transfer the clutter from my brain to paper, after which my mind thinks it doesn't have to think about it as much. This allows space and time for other thoughts and inspirations. And that can be an amazing thing. Over twenty years of journaling, I have experienced many times that, completely out of the blue, guidance and ideas start to come in once I have opened up the space they need.

One of my major influences and inspirations, and the architect behind my life-coach training, is Tony Robbins, the globally renowned transformational coach. He is worth checking out. His site says 'As people look to take a "time out" from their extra-busy lives, or to reflect on what's going on in the world, more and more are discovering the benefits of journaling. Tony Robbins himself has been keeping journals for as long as he can remember. They can help you see your progress, remember day-to-day events and focus on your future goals. They've certainly worked for Tony ... Journaling can actually help you be more productive, saving you time in the end. Whether you want to make sense of your busy life or pause and reflect, journaling has a wealth of benefits just waiting to be discovered.'

So, how to start? ... well, it's really simple, but the challenge is not to overthink it, or think that whatever comes out of your head and onto the paper has to make sense.

First, get yourself a special book, something beautiful and meaningful to you. I suggest you select it yourself, rather than accepting a gift chosen by someone else. I think it's worth taking the time to choose the right book, and for me this is where 'ye olde book shop' or stationery shop wins over online shopping. I buy one every December and I make the effort to go into the store to choose it using feel, touch, sight and smell. It has to be right for me, because it is going to hold important information, and I may keep it ... forever.

Once you have chosen your special book, find some quiet space, take a deep breath and begin. From my experience, the initial stuff often doesn't make sense. But that's fine, because whatever is meant to come out, is meant to comes out. Not unlike meditation, it's important to keep going without trying too hard or trying to analyse what is going on. Keep writing until it feels like there is nothing more to be expressed. The more you do this, and the more you combine it with meditation practice and all the other practices, the quicker it will be for the day's 'garbage' to pass out of your head, and for issues of greater depth and significance to your purpose to appear.

From my experience, it's worth going over what you have written at least once, especially if there are new ideas appearing that feel worth exploring. Otherwise, obsessing too much about what you have written may not be that useful; I would suggest you not continually read what you have written, and instead go out and take action.

4.7.2 Increase your awareness of your thinking, feelings and actions—and those of others

Our existence can be described as one of duality (see chapter three). We are capable of living and experiencing our 'normal' lives here on Planet Earth (our three-dimensional existence), but we also have the potential to stand away from ourselves and observe ourselves having this experience. Observance can take the form of thinking, thoughts and feeling about what we are thinking and feeling. This is essentially aligning consciously with our higher, or true spiritual self. In doing this we enhance our awareness of our human experience and especially how we are reacting to external events through our thoughts and feelings. This detached awareness allows us the potential for greater depth of reflection on why we are responding in certain ways, and thus the opportunity for growth, change, and the achievement of greater alignment with our true self and life purpose and happiness in this lifetime.

Although awareness of our thoughts is important, we need

to be vigilant of the ability of our ego , through our mind, to direct operations in a way that may not always be for our highest good. This is especially true when it comes to expanding our perspective and considering issues in a way that differs to how we have been brought up, which I earlier called our 'point of reference' (see section 3.6). The ego sees one of its primary roles to keep you safe, and it does that by trying to convince you, through your thoughts and your physical reactions, not to break away from the norm and not to take risks. The creation of fear is its most powerful weapon.

Feelings, however, are a strong indicator. Although the ego has some ability to use our mind to create a sense of trepidation and obstruct us doing certain things, we can still connect with our feelings to determine what is right for us at a deeper level. It is easier to quieten the mind and connect with your feelings when we meditate, and this is why this practice is so important. Therefore, when we are experiencing our human life and when we are observing ourselves experiencing our human life, it is important to be aware of our feelings. If it feels good at both levels, it is more likely to be aligned with your true self. If it doesn't feel good on one of the levels, or either of them, then there is work to be done to understand why—and to change what you are doing.

As we expand this increasing awareness over time, we are able to reflect on the consequences of our thoughts. Einstein maintained that our thoughts affect and create our world and life experience.

The world as we created it, is a process of our thinking.
It cannot be changed without changing our thinking
—Albert Einstein

Even if you don't believe this, by increasing your awareness of your thoughts and 'what should happen next', both for you and those affected by your presence, you might see patterns that support the idea that what you think is more significant for your life outcomes than has been generally accepted.

Extending this further to the concept of manifestation, we find multiple resources over the ages, and in particular in the past 100 years, that explore the idea that what you think and (more importantly) feel, can create your life outcomes. We have already noted the work of Wattle and Hill; more recently Rhonda Byrne's *The Secret* (Byrne, 2006) explored this idea further with a number of techniques and the film of the same name (Heriot, 2006), presented a number of well established personal development experts such as Bob Proctor, Jack Canfield and Lisa Nicholls, who explained how the law of attraction works, and how it can be used it to improve our lives.

Although the film received a degree of criticism, it does present powerful true stories that illustrate how thought and feeling can overcome adversity. For example, Cathy Goodman removed all traces of breast cancer in three months, without any radiation or chemotherapy, through the power of positive thought, will and laughter. In the period before this, her future husband Morris E Goodman, titled 'the Miracle Man', the survivor of a plane crash that left him apparently paralysed through most of his body and who was told by his doctors that he would never walk or speak again, strolled out of hospital unaided after nine months, healed by self-belief alone.

4.7.3 Breaking free from fear and despair (and social constructs)

More often than not, individuals' 'point of reference' prevents them from moving forward. This is the outcome of an upbringing that implanted in them a number of social, environmental and personal beliefs and traits that they believe cannot be changed. Which is not true. These beliefs manifest themselves as fear and sometimes despair (an idea that is explored further in the following sections). There is much written on the subject of fear, its origins and purpose. My abridged version comes in two parts, one based on medical science and one on the spiritual/human experience.

4.7.3.1 Fear: The link to the 'fight-or-flight' response. The medical explanation

Medicine says part of our basic design as human beings incorporates the ability to feel fear in order to respond to danger. So, when we experience acute stress, our amygdala (an area near the base of the brain that contributes to emotional processing) sends a distress signal to the hypothalamus, another area of the brain that functions like a command centre, communicating with the rest of the body through the autonomic nervous system, which controls such involuntary functions as breathing, blood pressure, heartbeat and the dilation or constriction of blood vessels and airways in the lungs.

This has two components, the sympathetic and the parasympathetic nervous system. The former functions like the accelerator in a car: it triggers the fight-or-flight response, providing the body with a burst of energy so it can respond to perceived dangers. The parasympathetic nervous system acts like a brake. It promotes the 'rest and digest' response that calms the body after the danger has passed.

After the amygdala sends a distress signal, the hypothalamus activates the sympathetic nervous system by sending signals to the adrenal glands. These respond by pumping the hormone adrenaline into the bloodstream. As this circulates, it brings on a number of physiological changes. The heart beats faster, pushing blood to the muscles, heart and other vital organs. Pulse rate and blood pressure go up. The person undergoing these changes starts to breathe more rapidly and small airways in the lungs dilate so they take in as much oxygen as possible. Extra oxygen is sent to the brain, increasing alertness. Sight, hearing, and other senses become sharper. Meanwhile, adrenaline also triggers the release of glucose and fats from temporary storage sites in the body. These flood into the bloodstream, supplying energy to all parts of the body.

All of these changes happen so quickly that people aren't aware of them. In fact, the wiring is so efficient that the amygdala and hypothalamus start this cascade before the brain's visual centres have had a chance to fully process what is happening. That's why people are able to jump out of the path of an oncoming car without thinking about what they are doing.

The spiritual explanation

Not every fearful situation involves imminent physical danger. As complex sentient beings, with complex social structures, some of our greatest anxieties can be centred around a perceived risk of embarrassment or failure, for example at work, in front of family and friends, rather than the need to deal with a predator chasing us across the savanna. However, our sense of anguish feels all too real and may trigger a 'flight' response, and also a 'fight' response, for example by motivating us to work harder.

When it comes to spiritual growth and evolution, fear can sometimes present as an entity in itself and can be extremely powerful if supplied with adequate energy, almost to the point where it can stop us from taking action to progress. It is said that fear is linked to ego, and as we have seen, ego typically tries to maintain a status quo that we know and feel comfortable with. Of course, ego is not really separate from us, but it can appear as an autonomous part of our subconscious ... the voice in our head that wants to reduce risk and keep us safe, in its own perception. It does not buy into the idea that taking risks to achieve a greater outcome is a valid reason for action. It only sees the risks that often accompany a change to the status quo, which it is designed to prevent. It is suggested by Jack Canfield (Canfield & Switzer, 2005) that some psychologists like to say that fear means:

- Fantasised
- Experiences
- Appearing
- Real

This supports the idea that fear is a creation of our own mind that can be reduced, removed or reframed in order to free ourselves of it's apparent control over us.

On Planet Earth right now, with our limited progression in spiritual growth on a mass scale, fear is having a good time. For many people, especially those living in the West, or in a traditional religious community, the idea of pursuing personal spiritual growth outside of the accepted paradigm can be very challenging. Practical spirituality is often hindered by a social environment that is less than supportive, for no other reasons that it considers the pursuit of your personal aligned goals to be 'different'. In the 1960s and 1970s, people pursuing a spiritual path, if not Buddhist monks, were often referred to as 'hippies' or 'weirdos'. Luckily, this has changed, but non-religious spirituality in a Western context at least, outside of religion, is still often considered 'alternative'.

So, in terms of spiritual growth, fear is to be acknowledged and then let go. It's important to remember that growth does not come through easy experiences, and the human experience model seems to be based on the paradigm that soul growth comes through embracing the opportunities that arise from challenge. So, to borrow a well-used phrase, we need to 'feel the fear and do it anyway', regardless of just how dire the potential consequences conjured by the fear machine appear to be. (Obviously, real risk of death and harm to self and others needs to be taken seriously and avoided.)

It is often said that fear reaches its peak just before a breakthrough. A similar expression is 'the darkest hour is just before dawn'. The fear and ego machine goes into overdrive as it begins to believe that it is losing control. Just before performing to a large audience, or running an important race, the sense of trepidation will often accelerate to extreme levels, manifesting in various physical symptoms such as shortness of breath, vomiting and a desire to go to the bathroom more often. All of these represent the fear/ego machine's attempts to stop you taking risks. We often experience similar symptoms when expanding our spiritual consciousness. A great slew of 'what ifs' appear in our minds, all of them designed to build the case that we should not be taking the risk. When this process conjures up all the unknowns, all the doubts and risks a new departure might bring, it is important to remember, again, the words of Martin Luther King, Jr: 'You don't have to see the whole staircase. Just take the first step'. Another relevant analogy from Jack Canfield describes a night-time car journey from San Francisco to New York, approximately 3,000 miles. When you leave San Francisco, you cannot see your destination because your headlights only shine 100 metres ahead, but that is okay, because you don't need to see every step of the whole journey, just what is immediately ahead of you. And the lights will continue to shine 100 metres ahead for the whole way, showing you what you need to see when you need to see it. The important thing is start the journey … and of course make sure your lights are working!

4.7.4 Despair: What it is, how to deal with it

Often times we find ourselves in what appears to be a pit of despair and self-pity, with no apparent route out. Everything seems forlorn and there doesn't appear to be a positive option to escape this. The triggers or causes of these feelings can range from the smallest to the most extreme set of circumstances, and although on some level we may be able to see that they should not deserve such an extreme emotional response, it is still difficult to escape them. Sometimes they last for a few hours, but it may be much longer periods.

For clarity, I am not talking about medically defined chronic conditions such as depression, although it is possible that some of the techniques mentioned below can alleviate its symptoms. So why do we have these moments? They are definitely an outcome of life stress with many possible causes: a lack of balance, poor mental and physical care, a lack of self-compassion, remaining in personal and work relationships that do not support us, a failure to step away from situations and reflect on them from places of quiet and calm and healthy environments, such as taking walks, exercising in nature, or swimming, especially in the sea. Laughter, especially with others, is also important in shifting perspective.

But is there a spiritual purpose or reason for despair? Well, perhaps. Sometimes going to a low point allows us to find a different perspective on an issue and maybe change our approach. This may be a small adjustment or maybe a radical shift, perhaps taking our lives in a different direction, more aligned with our true selves and life purposes. Canfield in his *The Success Principles* uses the analogy of an elastic band. The farther you pull it back, into the darkness and challenge, then when you let it go , the farther forward into the light, progress, wisdom and enlightenment you will end up. I love this idea.

The way to deal with the challenges and opportunities inherent in our human experience is to remember your dual nature: you are subject to experiences in the Matrix, but you also have the capacity to be outside it, observing your human self having those experience. This is not always easy, but if only for a moment you can cultivate the habit of shifting your perception to 'outside looking in', and then do it again and keep repeating it, you increase your chances of reducing the power of the energy that is attracted to the notion and generating feelings of despair. Distracting it and refusing to feed it, means it cannot survive and thus starts to dissipate.

Practical steps to achieve this begin with deep breathing exercises and meditation. This immediately increases the flow of oxygen to your brain and body, calms you down and starts to shift your focus. Through some meditation processes you can visualise the removal of stress, for example by expelling it when you breathe out, and inhaling beautiful white universal light when breathing in—a process of grounding and rebalancing and reducing the feeing and sense of despair.

Journaling is another positive way of extracting the myriad thoughts in your head in order to create the space for more positive energy, ideas and a more balanced perspective to flow in, as well as attracting guidance from your higher self and other sources, such as spirit guides. I find journaling an extremely powerful way to reduce almost immediately the apparent significance of an issue that has become stuck in my head. It's important to remember not to spend too much time reading what you have written down. It bears repeating that this will often appear to be gobbledygook, but stick with it and be open to whatever needs to flow out, for the process is more important than the details of what you produce. You might want to write these thoughts on a piece of paper that you can throw away, rather in your permanent journal.

As an illustration of how this has worked for some of the people who agreed to share their experiences in this book, consider the cases of Isabella and Shiela, who both found their young lives approaching points of extreme challenge for various different reasons,. Their stories showed how a crisis enabled them to reevaluate, rebalance and realign themselves with their true purpose, with the help of meditation, contact with nature, strengthened connection with their higher selves, spirit guides and other techniques.

Christina's Story

Receiving extra money from eBay

I am so happy and grateful that I now have more money available to me. I set a goal of increasing my income and truly believed that this is what will happen. Every day I give thanks for the extra money I am receiving every week, easily and effortlessly. Whilst I recited this mantra I always smiled and truly felt happy and grateful. This is what happened:

A friend of my brother-in-law was selling a car on eBay. It was a Mercedes and they put it on auction for £0.99. The description was hilarious and attracted a lot of attention, which in turn made the bids go massively high—right up to £150,000. The media were interested and the friend was interviewed on both UK and US TV. I was very focused on the bids and I was amazed to watch them keep climbing. I sent them a huge thank you for such a funny description as I had been feeling low with a cold and it had really cheered me up. I then shared their good fortune with all that I know and it was a topic of conversation daily.

This all led to me thinking I really should put items on eBay. I thought about it and wondered what and from nowhere came the thought—'go into the attic, look in box, look in flower fairy tin and get girl guide badges'. Well, this thought was so random that I had to follow it. Sure enough, in a box, in the flower fairy tin, were my girl guide badges, so I put them on eBay for £0.99. People started bidding and they sold. I then asked 'what next?' and again a random thought: 'in attic – tea set from childhood'. Sure enough, there it was and I washed it—sorted it out—there were lots of different bits of tea sets—and put it up for £0.99. The bidding went really well and I sold it for £10.50.

Since then, I have continued to allow myself to be guided what to put on eBay and I have now received over £200 from selling items that I have had here in my home. The whole process is very easy and very effortless. Thank you, thank you, thank you!

Receiving more money for the work I'm already doing

I set an intention of receiving more money easily and effortlessly. I did not know how this would happen but I just positively set the intention and let the thought go.

And here is what happened: I was driving along, and I suddenly wondered if I was getting paid the right amount for one of my teaching jobs—I am getting more from one job for fewer hours which made me question it. It is not something that ever crossed my mind before, and then there it was, planted in my mind.

I approached the business adviser at school and asked her to look into it. It was met harshly at first, but I kept reminding myself that I deserved this money. Anyway, it worked out that they hadn't been paying me for 25 minutes of work a week.

All was resolved easily, amicably and effortlessly and the school has agreed to pay me an extra £40 a month, and I do not have to do anything other than what I was already doing. I got my payslip today and before this increase I notice there was an extra £65. Therefore my total increase in pay from this job is over £100 a month.

Thank you. Thank you. Thank you.

4.8 Increase your awareness of your true past and your reality ... inside and outside the Matrix

This section explores the ideas of alternative earth and human histories, the idea of intelligent design, and what this means for your life journey from a practical daily perspective: for example, observing your human be-ing from inside and outside the Matrix. Anthony shares some more details around his own journey and how he engages with the realm of spiritual support (outside the matrix) to achieve alignment and support purpose.

4.8.1 The true past

Understanding our true human history, as outlined in chapter three, helps us to set in context our current reality, and supports the idea that we are living in a constructed three-dimensional reality, created for the development and growth of our spirit and soul, which is part of all that is, or the universal life force, or god.

To recap the ideas that I first came across as I started my awakening at the age of twenty-two when reading *The Only Planet of Choice*, the 'accepted' version of our Earth history is very limited. Rather than being a small unique planet, alone and on the edge of a galaxy, we are in fact living on a planet that has been, and still is, connected to other beings from across the cosmos, our universe and other universes. Importantly, that means that what happens here matters.

Every ancient and native culture has embedded within their origin story the idea that they were created by another being of some sort, usually 'Sky Beings' of one sort or another, and that they were also given knowledge and shown how to develop in all aspects of their lives, from other beings that came from the sky, who then left, see *Chariots of the Gods: Unsolved Mysteries of the Past* (Von Däniken, 1968). This theory is supported by numerous ancient texts and customs, ancient oral stories and multiple identical ancient structures that exists all over the world, most notably, perhaps, the pyramids of Egypt, Mexico and other parts of South America, China, Asia, Europe and all over the world.

Throughout our recorded history, we have many stories, some found in the Christian Bible, that have long been thought to be legends and myths, for example, Noah's Ark and the Great Flood. Interestingly, many non-Christian traditions that have similar stories regard them as records of historical fact. And science is now coming to the party with the emergence of data, proven using the long-established scientific method, which is beginning to support their reinterpretation of so-called science fiction as science fact. A great example is the Younger Dryas. In his book *America Before: The Key to Earth's Lost Civilization* (Hancock, 2019), international bestselling author Graham Hancock explores the idea of an advanced civilization lost to history in the global cataclysm that ended the last Ice Age. He suggests that for some decades it has been generally accepted that a global cataclysm occurred around 12,800 years ago at the onset of a mysterious period of earth changes and climate instability known to geologists as the Younger Dryas. Drawing on the latest archaeological and DNA evidence, Hancock explains how since 2007 a group of more than sixty scientists, publishing in leading peer-reviewed journals, have presented evidence linking the cataclysm to a disintegrating comet that crossed the orbit of the earth 12,800 years ago and bombarded our planet with a swarm of fragments, some more than a kilometre in diameter. Although the comet hypothesis remains controversial, and a number of scientists favour other explanations, it is common ground that a global cataclysm did indeed occur, and caused an immense flood, as large areas of the ice caps suddenly melted and swaths of the planet were swept clean by a deluge. At the same time as global sea-levels rose, the Gulf Stream was stopped in its tracks and the world was plunged into a deep freeze that lasted 1,200 years. It was the end of the former age of the earth, the Pleistocene, and the beginning of our own epoch, the Holocene. It is the thesis of *America Before* that an advanced civilization, hitherto the stuff of myth and legend, was lost to history.

It is suggested that this period aligns very accurately with the idea of the flood myths and major rapid flooding across the globe that led to a significant reduction in archaeological evidence of human activity. The flood-myth occurs in the oral and written traditions of multiple cultures worldwide including Noah (the Hebrew Bible), Nuh (Islam), Mavantara-sandhya (Hinduism), Gun-Yu (Chinese mythology), Deucalion and Pyrrha (Greek mythology), Bergelmir (Norse mythology) and Cessair (Irish mythology). The story is also repeated among the first nation people of Hawaii, the K'iche' and Mayan peoples in Mesoamerica, the Lac Courte Oreilles Ojibwa people of North America, the Muisca and Cañari Confederation in South America and some first nation peoples in Australia.

From this period onwards in the archaeological record we begin to see significant increase in human activity across the globe, new cultures evolving along with high culture and art and technology. Within this Neolithic period (12,000 BP to 6,500 BP) and later, we begin to see the construction of significant megalithic structures all over the world, some showing incredible engineering technology that accepted history suggests was invented only in the past 200 years. And many of them are connected to the stars: for example, the three major pyramids of the Giza Plateau in Egypt align with the three stars of Orion's belt as they appeared in 12,000 BP (Bauval, 1989) and major structures at Teotihuacan, Mexico, are similarly aligned with Orion's belt, as seen from Earth in that era.

These ideas are important because they expand your consciousness. Even if they cannot be proven using the accepted methods of science and archaeology, that does not mean they are not based on truth as yet to be determined. In considering these and other ideas outside the norm, it is important to think about how the scientific professions work. The world of academia functions through a process of peer review and uses the established history of what has gone before as the starting position when considering proposed changes, through new theories. Career progression, funding and the economic stability and assurance of academics and their families therefore relies on their publishing in front of their peers and generally working within the accepted norms of their professional world. Stepping outside of that world in any radical sense and challenging the norms is a potentially dangerous and career-ending approach to their lives. So, unless they have secured independent funding, the incentives for academics to push the boundaries are limited. Partly for these reasons, when established archaeology is asked to explain technologically advanced findings such as the megalithic stone structures at Puma Punku, near Tiwanacu in Boliva, which shows signs of being manufactured by machine tools thousands of years ago, or similar megalithic stone structures at Sacsayhuaman in Cusco, Peru, which appeared to have been melted and fused together, they chose to ignore the issue. It cannot be fitted into the accepted timeline of human development and it is therefore too risky, personally and professionally, to explore the idea that they may have been created in a technological environment considered impossible by the accepted historical record.

Multiple ancient cultures around the world have in their

lore a story of a god or Sky Beings that created humans or gave them knowledge that advanced their cultures. These stories are present world wide and it is striking how often the gods have similar anatomical features. Some appear to have the ability to fly, such as the Anunnaki in ancient Sumerian mythology and Quetzalcóatl, the plumed serpent, in Mexico. Established archaeology struggles with this because without an established historical story that links these cultures across the world and across time with travel and cultural integration, then all they have is the idea of incredible coincidence. This is the same explanation often given for the existence of ancient pyramids all over the world, with striking similarities in design across continents, at a time when apparently humankind was not travelling across the planet.

This approach is not new for Planet Earth of course. In the seventeenth century, Galileo stood trial for challenging the Roman Catholic-administered belief that the Sun and the universe revolved around the Earth. Eventually they had to change their minds on that one!

So, what is important is to be open to the possibility that what you read in the accepted channels of communication, news, government, school, especially around history and your existence on Earth, may not be the full story. Stay open, keep your mind clear, and go and explore. This will raise your vibration and expand your consciousness and leave yourself open to receive what you need to receive for your life journey. Go check out the History Channel, go into a bookshop, check online for mind-bending, history-bending, reality-changing books. You might find that the truth IS out there.

On the subject of conspiracy theories, they can be useful to shift you out of a stuck paradigm, but take care. They can be interesting, fun, thought-provoking and amusing, but I believe they can also become a paradigm in themselves, and can probably make you unwell if you allow yourself to get too drawn into them. The risk is that you start to lose touch with your common sense, or even a healthy reality. If you start to see conspiracy theories within conspiracy theories within conspiracy theories, then it's probably time to turn off the phone, shut down the computer, put away the book and go for a very long walk—possibly for a few weeks!

Having been somewhat obsessed by these in my younger years, as I got older and observed the actions of certain large bodies, especially public organisations and governments here in the UK, I began to suspect that these organisations didn't have the capacity to orchestrate mass-manipulation of the populace. That's not to say there aren't clever manipulating types operating at the highest level—take for example what we now know about the Brexit referendum and the 2016 US presidential election—but not everything in life is being controlled by shadowy figures.

From a practical spirituality perspective, researching and being aware of these issues, for example through exploring the ancient alien/astronaut and advanced ancient civilisation ideas, is a good way to raise your consciousness to a wider galactic and universal community and a deeper and older human backstory. Anything that stretches your consciousness is positive to handle change, and possibly to lead it, too. Be aware of any resistance you find to exploring these ideas and explore why. Step outside of the Matrix, your conscious self, and feel where that resistance is coming from. Is it from the programming of your upbringing and the media you watched all your life, or is it something else? Explore the idea of ancient peoples seemingly transporting 20-tonne megaliths over great distances, and ask yourself how you feel about the official position on how they were moved and why.

In this age where the 'truth' is a perspective, I believe for your human experience the only thing you can do is 'feel' your way to your truth. Remember, almost everything that comes to you through your TV, newspaper, mobile phone or other media route has an agenda behind it. No exceptions!

As you align your journey, meditate and connect with yourself more, then information that is important to you will become visible, because it will support the achievement of your purpose.

As I mentioned in chapter three, we have come willingly (at a soul level) into this environment to try to remember why we are here and ultimately to help humanity to move forward, into the light. This requires courage and compassion but those of us consciously awake are not alone and connection with tribe is extremely important to help you achieve your purpose whilst you are here.

4.8.2 Human evolution—by design?

Within the idea of exploring our true past, what appears all over the world, through history and the historiography of oral traditions, cave art, megalithic structures and archaeology, is the idea of advanced technology on Earth in the ancient past. The existence of similar stories, art and cultural practices across the globe suggest that these advanced civilisations had the ability to make contact with peoples across the world, implying they had the power of flight. There is much that can be explored around this idea, one version of which is the ancient astronaut theory proposed by Erich Von Däniken in the 1960s and is now being adopted, if tentatively, by some mainstream scientists, archaeologists and engineers. The 'what' in these stories is fascinating, but of more importance, I believe, is the 'why'.

Mesopotamia, the land between the Tigris and Euphrates rivers—modern-day Iraq, Kuwait, Turkey and Syria—is considered to be the site of the first neolithic revolution that took place around 12,000 BP. This is where some of the most important developments in human history occurred, including the invention of the wheel, the planting of the first cereal crops and the development of cursive script, mathematics, astronomy and agriculture.

The accepted story is that this just happened. Humanity suddenly evolved from hunter–gatherers and cave dwellers to farmers. The alternative history is that this area was occupied by a non-earth species called the Annunaki who came to Earth to mine minerals, especially gold. They used advanced genetic technology to create the modern human race, homo sapiens sapiens, using creatures they found already here on Earth, thereby creating a workforce for themselves.

Other stories, embedded in the oral traditions of multiple cultures, tell of sky people who came to Earth to help humanity advance technologically and spiritually, teaching science, agriculture and astronomy. Shamans, priestesses and holy people were said to have gained this knowledge and used it to help their people. Eventually, the sky people left, presumably returning to their home planets, but leaving traces of the same messages, names and architecture across the globe and in the human psyche—in stories and structures such as pyramids and legends of the bird-related creatures/humanoids/feathered gods such as Quetzalcóatl and Huitzilopochtli (Mexico),

Apkallu (Iraq) and Horus (Egypt).

Again, the stories and details are fascinating and there are sources that can be explored to satisfy your appetite to know more in this area, starting with the work of Graham Hancock. However, the importance of this narrative for practical spirituality is that it supports the idea of human experience being under a degree of guardianship—that the journey that we humans have travelled as a species has been guided by 'others' who, at times, taught us better ways to live, and possibly even gave us the rules of our society (one example being Moses receiving the Ten Commandments from 'on high'). Perhaps the most disconcerting idea for some people is the notion that our very presence on Earth is by design at the DNA level—that we did not evolve naturally from apes or an earlier version of man, which is why the so-called 'missing link' does not exist in the way mainstream science thinks it should. Have you ever stopped to wonder how and why a dark-skinned humanoid species originating in Africa would eventually evolve into pale-skinned races with significantly differing physical traits? Could the influence of environment alone really have created these significant changes, even over hundreds of thousands of years? I have always struggled with this idea. It just doesn't make sense to me.

So, we exist in an environment that has in effect been created and we are, and have always been, far more connected to the rest of the universe than we could ever have imagined. This connection will continue and as 'full disclosure' happens and so-called aliens are visible on our TVs and smartphones, and we truly know we are not alone in the universe, we will become aware of just how connected we truly are to the rest of existence and also how common hybrid human species really are across the universe. We will probably also find that there are multiple races across the galaxies who look like us. Why? Because their ancestors' DNA was used to create ours. As the Bible suggests, we are 'created in the image of our father'.

4.8.3 Living inside and outside matrix

All of these stepping stones lead up to the final idea—which may still be considered a leap—that not only are we a created species, but that our existence itself is not as real as it feels. In section 3.4 we explored the idea that we are living in a created reality that is similar in principle to that portrayed in the movie *The Matrix*. It is a construct that includes the aliens and artifacts and the Younger Dryas, and was created in order for our soul (and by extension god or existence) to know itself. In other words, the creation of souls and spirits and their incarnation into this universe is a way for that universe to understand itself and grow. And growth comes from challenge.

When we sleep we return to spirit, which is our normal status. When we die, we also return to spirit—but as we are spirit all the time, perhaps it is more accurate to say it is the end of the physical incarnation of our soul in that particular body. Our soul may incarnate in multiple bodies at the same time. Some people suggest that past life regression is actually a connection with alternative beings in your soul group, because reincarnation doesn't exist. We don't die and come back round again.

For practical spirituality this idea is key to understanding the purpose of the human experience and thus working out why you're here and what you should be doing with the time and the opportunity that you have. I believe that being awake to this idea gives you the potential to live within the

Matrix and outside, too. By being inside, we experience the real issues, challenges and joys of human life; by being outside, we are observing our responses to all of these external factors, including the decisions we make and how we respond to their consequences. Thus, you are not only living your growth opportunities, but you are observing them at the same time. I believe that this ability is what allows us to improve our compassion and empathy for ourselves and for others, because it enables us to reflect on the actions of others from their perspectives, not just our own. Similarly, it allows greater self-compassion because it enables us to observe our own feelings and actions as observers, and thus not beat ourselves up too much when we make mistakes or things don't go as we would have wanted them to.

4.8.4 Increase your knowledge of daily events—but don't watch the news!

This heading sounds contradictory, but there is an important message here about energy, the Earth-bound collective consciousness and the nature of our global media. In essence, although global communications bring undoubted benefits to our planet, the twenty-four-hour outpouring of negative news is not good for most people's mental health. The nature of news reporting appears to be about extending the truth to create story of interest, and it appears that the human race is currently more interested in what might go wrong and how much worse things might get than any positive message.

I am not suggesting that news and social media does not have an important role to play, for example by raising awareness of climate change and uncovering and sharing the abuses of those in power over the years. However, the news also plays to our basic fears and has created an energy field that is low vibration and negative. It is also strangely addictive. Research led by Graham Davey, emeritus professor of psychology at the University of Sussex, has shown that 'not only are negatively valanced news broadcasts likely to make you sadder and more anxious, they are also likely to exacerbate your own personal worries and anxieties'. So, from a practical spirituality perspective, it is probably healthy to restrict ourselves to a little news, not very often, and absorb it while being consciously aware of the energy associated it. How, then, should we find out what's going on—and why should we bother?

Being awake to global developments is important because of the opportunities that might arise to support your own journey. The global churn and chaos since 2016 has clearly reflected major change in the balance of energies here in our reality, and signifies an accelerating destabilisation of the status quo. I believe this signals the labour pains of humanity's next evolutionary leap. This may take another two or three decades to come about, but something major is definitely happening on multiple levels of existence. It is therefore important to be observant, but not obsessed, by what is happening in the world.

Staying true to finding and living your purpose remains the key to living a practically spiritual life. Look into documentaries, occasionally the news, occasionally social media, connect with local groups and energy healers and light workers. Connect with what resonates with you, but always be cognisant of the source and possible motivations of anything that you see or receive, and do not become obsessed. Develop your tools for connecting with your higher self to decide whether something is aligned with your higher good, such as using the sacral chakra or gut feeling. Science is regularly announcing findings that support hitherto 'legendary' spiritual ideas. Connect with these because they support raising the vibration of human consciousness. The Gaia organisation (Gaia, 2017) is a good place to check out.

Anthony's story

I was baptised in a Catholic church (my father's decision) in the late 1960s and except for my younger sisters' christening a few years later, my next visit to such a place was a Methodist church when I was about seven years old—my grandparent's church. This, along with English school-based religious education, religious spirituality helped me over my childhood and teenage years to form a fairly dim view of this rather confusing, rule-driven, and often contradictory part of so many people's life.

So, I grew up in an environment of understanding of the Bible stories and a general acceptance that the parables probably made a lot of sense. At the same time, religion was not overt in our lives, and for many years it was just 'something we had to do' every Sunday, until we could find a way of getting out of it. By my mid-teens I was working on Sunday mornings and church attendance was a thing of the past. It wasn't until many years later that I began to really understand religion and, in my perception, its journey from a fairly decent set of guidance and principles on how to live life and treat others with compassion, to what it is today—which often contradicts its founding principles. But … it still has a value.

Describe your spirituality

I 'know' I'm an incarnation in this three-dimensional existence of my higher self, soul and spirit, and that I'm experiencing the opportunities for growth that come through challenge. I know that my natural state is spirit. Therefore, my spirituality describes how I connect with my true self in order to be consciously connected and aware of, and with, all that is and to receive guidance and retain alignment with my true self and purpose.

What is your earliest memory of awakening?

In my early 20s my corporate life started at almost the exact same time as my conscious spiritual journey. For me it began with a book called *The Only Planet of Choice*, which was brought to my attention by my new neighbour and now long-term friend, who happened to be a crop circle researcher.

How did you feel? What challenges did you face?

This new knowledge was very exciting and at the same time slightly scary (alien abductions, etc). It did not align at all with my emerging corporate life, or the knowledge from my upbringing, so it was an almost secret 'other' awareness that certainly could not be discussed amongst colleagues and friends in the 1990s UK.

What happened next?

The book was my introduction to the idea of their being 'something else' and an alternative explanation to our human existence, backstory and purpose. The book and my time with my friend led me to explore meditation, crop circles, extraterrestrials and to begin to have real energy experiences, for example, by touching the megoliths at Stonehenge and Avebury. Mind body and spirit shops came onto my radar and I began a lifelong, expensive habit of buying as many books as I could that I felt drawn to. I also started exploring astrological predictions through The Astrology Shop in Covent Garden, London.

Through my massive consumption of books at this time I studied reincarnation, past lives, Buddhism, ancient aliens, alternative human histories and meditation techniques. I also allowed myself to be engrossed in government/alien cover-ups, faked moon landings and related conspiracy theories and movies that presented these ideas (such as *Capricorn One*).

I practised forms of meditation, These were sporadic and frustrating, as I seemed unable to stop all the clutter in my mind. I still managed to have some 'energy experiences' during this time, but the frustration also grew as I was still believing that I needed to 'empty' my mind.

My professional career and my social life progressed well, and tended to eclipse my spiritual journey. However, my intuition that there was more to life remained constant, if a little lacking in attention. Eventually, I created my own renewable energy business and was approached to lead an investment project in New Zealand. I spent six years there, which is where my spiritual calling kicked back in, thanks to my introduction to reiki energy healing.

Through my journey I have been inspired by much wisdom, including that offered by Tony Robbins, Jack

Canfield, Michael Beckwith, a number of collaborators in Mind Valley and many more people, events, relationships, as well as self-reflection and insights.

A key moment?

Twenty years later, having continued my professional corporate progression, experienced personal growth as a father and husband, and continued my spiritual growth through books, and some online courses and interactions, I attended my first reiki session as a client in Wellington, New Zealand. This led to my attunements as a healer, the use of reiki for self-healing and also for others.

Back in the UK a few years later, I took my attunements again and then in 2019 completed my reiki master course. This was a key moment for me, coming about four months after I finally crystalised my life purpose as raising the vibration of human consciousness, and to do this in part through practising and teaching reiki energy healing, and through writing, speaking and supporting others as a spiritual life coach.

What does your spiritual day/week look like now?

- I meditate every morning for thirty minutes. If I don't, my day can be a challenge.
- I try consciously to do only those things that are aligned with my purpose and avoid becoming drawn into other's energy if it doesn't resonate with mine.
- I regularly visit places in nature to recharge and reconnect (through meditation), for example, the South

Downs, which has a ley line from Eastbourne to Glastonbury.

- I connect with spirit guides and my higher self regularly if I need to ask for help.
- I continue to develop my practice, to learn and to continue to grow.
- I endeavour to be grateful for everything I have and for the opportunity that challenges represent.
- I offer reiki healing and practical spirituality coaching to those who resonate with these things.

And how do you feel now?

I see my first fifty years as two phases that were preparation and prelude to my third and final phase—where I get to give back. This latest stage is no easier than the previous two, but the fact that I have found my purpose means that I can focus my activities and decisions on that which aligns with it, and can be aware, with the help of my spiritual practice, of that which does not. I feel blessed to have awareness of the duality of my existence, which allows me to be present inside the Matrix while observing my responses and reactions from outside, too.

What have you learned about your practical spirituality and the human experience?

- Life is not easy, by design. But it is full of wonder.
- By raising your awareness, you raise your vibration, and that makes easier the connection with and awareness of the universal energy of 'all that is'. Creating

meditative states is absolutely key to this.

- The circumstances of your birth and childhood were designed to set your personal point of reference, from which you base your growth opportunities for the rest of your life. There are no coincidences.
- Practical spirituality, for most of us, requires a degree of selflessness and self-compassion, especially for those of us in a family structure. But other people's lack of understanding of your spiritual needs, the nature of your journey and the difficulty we encounter when describing matters of faith are not reasons to not pursue that which you need to.
- It's important to take action—and risks!

4.9 Explore your life purpose: seek alignment with your truth

In this section we explore the idea of life purpose(s)—finding yours and living it (them). Estelle shares with us her lifelong engagement with spirituality, from inherited multi-generational spiritual practice, and an astute awareness of her sense of self and her healing abilities as part of her continuing personal journey.

4.9.1 Explore your life purpose

In chapter three, we touched on the idea of a life purpose: what it is, and whether everyone has one. Within the context of my belief in the human experience paradigm (see chapter 3.2), I would say the answer is yes, we all have at least one, because we were incarnated into this life to find it, and through it to support our soul's desire to grow. Usually this comes though challenge, and Planet Earth and our three-dimensional universe certainly creates multiple opportunities for that.

So, your purpose is unique to you. In Japanese this is called *ikigai* (Garcia & Miralles, 2016).You may have more than one during your life, and they might change to reflect its phases. It took fifty-two years to understand my own, but I needed those challenges and opportunities to be able to achieve it.

An internet search for 'how to find your life purpose' will produce numerous results. In principle, they follow a similar approach that requires you to 'go inside', connect with your higher self, possibly through meditation, and identify that which gives you your highest excitement, your passion.

This is about feeling, not thinking. The thing that you could do all day, because it is your passion, not just because it makes you lots of money or fame or anything else. I suggest you take the time to explore different approaches and journal and meditate on this issue. Exercises that help you to remove limiting belief are also powerful supporting tools, because your mind can come up with lots of reasons why what comes through cannot be your passion, because there is no way that you could achieve it. Remember the human experience is a challenge by design, so it's quite likely that achieving your true purpose and passion will come with hurdles to negotiate along the way.

A common approach to exploring your true purpose is to:

- Write down everything that you do in life and everything that you think you would like do.
- Sit seriously with this list and meditate on it. Consider each item and be aware of how you feel about it. Try to gauge which make you feel more excited than others, at the deepest level that you can feel. Be aware of anything that came into the list that was unusual to your life, that you had never considered

before. Do not ignore or discard anything at this stage. This will allow you to order your list into favourites and less favourites.

- The next step is to take the top ten favourites and do the feeling exercise again, re-ordering them in terms of more or less favour; see if the list remains in the same order.
- When you've done this, take the top five and repeat the exercise.
- When you have these in order—do not take any big decisions. Sit with them for a few days, maybe a few weeks, meditate, explore them in whatever way you want (perhaps by research, or talking to friends and colleagues), and then run the exercise again and see what order they produce.

If the order changes, be aware why. If there are items that you have now decided you don't want to progress, cross them out and create a revised list. During this period, be aware of what comes into your visibility. Be conscious of synchronicities and odd events that take place that support your list. This is the universe helping you out! From my experience it is useful to be aware that what comes to you isn't always a suggestion from higher source to do a particular thing, it's usually more of the presentation of a choice or something to ponder, such as: 'What do you feel about this? Does it resonate with you?' That's why it's important not to make rash judgments; be still, meditate, go into the countryside, the sea and special energy places with your questions and be open to whatever needs to come up for you.

- Finally, it's time to take action. Take your top idea, expand your research and explore everything about it. Visualise yourself doing and being it, draft a route map out of how you could get there from your life today. Don't get hung up on the hurdles; stay positive, preserve the good feelings you have about achieving that goal as you write down possible journeysto reach it. This isn't necessarily the path that you'll take, so try not to get too hung up on the details.

It's important to do this because you are creating and enhancing your intent to achieve your goal, and if it feels good on a deep level, then it's probably aligned with your true purpose. The 'how' you get there is the universe's job—which it can do, with a little help from you. All you have to do is to create situations in which it can support you in your three-dimensional world.

I appreciate this is a simplified approach, and unfortunately the longer we have been on Planet Earth, the more personal baggage and limiting beliefs we accumulate, which often works to prevent us finding our purpose and achieve alignment. This process of working through everything that is stopping you moving forward may be considerable. If, like me, you have the usual responsibilities of a middle-aged person—a mortgage, children, and so on—then it could be that your sense of purpose may appear financially ludicrous, or self-centred in relation to your family and those who depend on you.

The support I give as a spiritual life coach helps people work through these issues. Sometimes I help them to reframe, sometimes to explore the difference between the perceived catastrophe of changing their lives to the possible okayness of transcending through a series of steps. This may take place over a period of years, enabling them to achieve their goals in a way that feels manageable for them and those around them. For others, this change can be rapid and radical. The internet is crowded with people offering routes to your purpose—too many to list here. Some take a spiritual approach; others have a more pragmatic list-type approach similar to my example above; others take alternative routes to the same destination.

The important thing is to find what works for you. That might involve a spiritual life coach who can guide you through the initial steps, and act as a sounding board as you develop your ideas and work through identifying and reducing the impact of your limiting beliefs. It is important to note that this exercise might take you through a series of steps and ideas that create a great deal of excitement in you at first but are not necessarily your life purpose.

This was my experience, and only in hindsight can I see that they reflected real needs I had at the time. This period lasted about three years, and it helped me to realise what I didn't want to do and what wasn't actually my passion. I could do them, and reasonably well, but they did not 'float my boat'. These were valuable lessons and for many of you that feel you have a billion things in your head that you would like to do, be assured that this situation is quite common, and be warned that it may not be easy to find the one or two or maybe three options that will support your purpose and alignment and your reasons for being here. This is a case where the journey is as important as the destination.

Here I want to mention that an ancient mechanism that may help you to establish your life purpose is the Akashic records. This is described in the next section.

4.9.2 Access your Akashic records

The Akashic records (from the Sanskrit ākāśa, meaning 'sky', 'space', or 'æther') are sometimes described as the memory of nature. The subtle matter that composes the different planes of the cosmos have the ability to receive and record impressions of everything that happens on the terrestrial plane. These records, which can be seen by clairvoyants, are a universal compendium of all events, thoughts, words, emotions and intents that have occurred in the past, present, or future to all entities and life forms. They are believed by theosophists to be encoded in a non-physical plane of existence known as the mental plane. Modern-day energy healers such as Jeffrey Allen and Mackenzie Grant offer guidance in ways to access your Akashic records and use them to assist in determining your purpose and achieving an aligned life.

According to Grant, 'we all have a "soul point", a connection to the source of our highest potential and greatest good that is communicating energetically with us, even through the noise of our human life.' She offers to 'access your Akashic records and the wisdom and guidance of your highest self and soul guides, who are ready to help you step back into the flow of life that you dreamed of as a child, when you were more connected to your purpose and unafraid'. She adds that 'when we are in alignment with our soul and the energetic flow emanating from that point, we are living in balance—physically, mentally, spiritually. When we listen to and act on our soul's true messages, we manifest everything we need, release what no longer serves us and reclaim our soul's aliveness and excitement for this one, precious life'.

Estelle's story[5]

Describe your spirituality

My spirituality is a deep love and respect for all living things on our planet. It is a deep understanding and ongoing investigation into who I truly am. For me, it

5 Estelle Coughlan, www.thelondonsoundhealer.co.uk

is about deciphering why I am here, and what I am I here to do. How can I leave the world a better place?

My spirituality is a constant journey of the soul, that will never end. It is about tuning into my inner knowing and finding the best methods for me to access this. This deep knowing brings me great purpose and peace, I am not sure where I would be without it. Very lost, I imagine.

I have a name, a life, an identity; but I know I am, and we are all are, so much more than these facts, and what is directly in front of us. Spirituality is about opening our eyes and our minds, it is about embracing love, kindness and forgiveness and journeying back to who we truly are. As babies, we were all born divine, and that divine soul is still there within us waiting to be rediscovered and rebirthed.

What is your earliest memory of spiritual awakening?

I have had many psychic experiences throughout my life, and from a young age I was always taught to tune into that and listen to my intuition. My family are all deeply spiritual, and I was even named after a psychic that my grandmother and aunt had visited. My mother and grandmother are spiritual healers, and my dad is deeply intuitive and psychic.

Our house was always full of esoteric books and lively discussions. Everyone in my family is very open minded, and discussions on Atlantis, what really lay beneath the Sphinx, inner Earth, psychic phenomena, ancient hidden history and working with energy, etc,

etc, were all part of daily life alongside more day-to-day discussions. In fact, when I go to my parents' house now, I am pretty blown away by the selection of esoteric and mystical books they have owned for decades, some even inherited from my grandparents and other family members.

My mum studied astrology for many years to a very deep level when I was growing up, so having planetary discussions was also part of the norm. We would often attend mind, body and spirit events, and I still have the beautiful crystals and tarot cards that my mum bought for me when I was young.

How did you feel? What challenges did you face?

My spirituality and faith have always been things that gave me great strength and got me through difficult times. Growing up in London, lots of my friends had similar interests, and we would spend our weekends in our teens looking at esoteric books and buying crystals in Mysteries in Covent Garden, which was a new age Aladdin's cave, or having card readings in Camden Town. This was all fun, and it bonded us.

I have always been an avid reader, and it was around this time that my mum bought me a book by Shakti Gawain called *Creative Visualisation*. This was pretty much a precursor to many mainstream books now such as *The Secret*. Through this book, I learned about visualisation, manifestation and about using mantras. In fact, the mantra that I started using at this time I still use to this day, and it has helped me so much in challenging times.

Another book that deeply moved me was a Buddhist book on vegetarianism that I was given in the street by a Buddhist monk when I was at university. I remember going home, sitting on my bed and reading the whole book in one day, and I cried and cried.

I had always been unable to eat meat and fish as it just seemed so wrong to me to be eating a living creature. The book covered in depth the economic and environmental reasons, in addition to the humane reasons, for not eating a living being. This really made me see the world in a different light, and how certain living beings are treated. It made me deeply sad.

What happened next?

I have carried on with my studies and interests at a deep level all my life, but there have been times when I have diverged and got caught up in the hamster wheel of life.

School, university and then setting out on the corporate ladder were all big distractions to my spirituality, although they have also proved vital in my life experience and learning.

In my early thirties, I had a senior marketing role, and on paper it looked like I was doing great. I had wonderful friends and family, I was married and had a lovely home with a great career. In practice, I was working exhausting hours and weekends, I had no energy to see any of my friends as I was so burnt out, and I was utterly depleted by the negative politics in the company in which I was working. I also realised that whatever I earned was irrelevant, as I always managed to spend it all.

It was at this point I realised I was a complete slave to the system, and I just did not want to be part of it anymore. What was the point of my life if this was all I was going to do? Who was I helping? No one, and certainly not myself.

I handed in my notice, and felt a huge weight lifted off my shoulders. I could start being me again.

A key moment?

A few years ago, I decided that I really needed to tune into my life's purpose. I wanted to help the planet and lead a good and meaningful life. How was I to do that?

I had been reading the books *Journey of Souls*, and *Destiny of Souls* by Dr Michael Newton. As opposed to just being books on regression, Dr Newton's work regressed subjects to a soul level, to help the souls understand why they were choosing their lives, and what were their purposes. These books really expanded my thinking to a soul level, and I was able to view myself from a different perspective.

I found a hypnotherapist who had been trained by Dr Newton himself, who specialised in life between lives regression. On the first of two sessions, I was asked to be shown my life on earth that has been most relevant to my life now. I was a Shaman in Central America, and I saw and felt every detail of that life, from where I lived and worked with plants, to how I felt and helped the local community. I felt deep contentment in that life.

Most importantly, I clearly saw my purpose in this life, and why I had chosen to incarnate again at this time.

Music has always been a deep passion of mine, and

for many years I had been dreaming, and sometimes waking up surrounded by the most beautiful music I had ever heard. Once when I was unwell, I woke up with the singing of what sounded like angels, and the most beautiful chandelier I had ever seen hanging above me. It remained with me for many minutes, and it was a divine experience I will never forget. I always felt instinctively that my destiny and what I should be doing was to do with music, sound, energy and healing.

My life between lives regression clearly showed this path. There was no looking back from this, and my training as a sound healer, in shamanism and as a reiki master has been transformational. We are vibrational beings, and we have the power to transform and heal with sound. It also allows us to attune to our higher self and feel connected to ourselves and others at a profound level.

What does your spiritual day/week look like now?

Meditation and gratitude are an important part of my day. I tend to meditate upon waking and practise gratitude at the end of the day. I also ask my children three things that they have had gratitude for in their day. This process is scientifically proven to raise a person's vibration, and I love doing this with my children as I often learn something about their day that may have never come up in conversation.

I ground and try to connect with source energy throughout the day, almost like a reset. I imagine my feet growing like the roots of a tree into Mother Earth, and I also envisage my crown chakra opening and connecting with my higher self, as though I am in a pillar of light, connected to the universe.

I check in with spirit as much as I can, and I always ask for help when needed. This may mean asking for protection if I am going on a journey, or if I am encountering a difficult situation. I have a power animal, who is always there for me to ask for help when I need her. I always listen to my intuition closely, and if I have a specific question or worry, I shamanically journey. This involves drumming between four to seven beats per second, to bring the brain into theta state. This takes me to another realm of consciousness, where I am able to see a situation, often from a different perspective, and gain guidance and help.

And how do you feel now?

We are in a time of great change and new understandings. Hidden histories and ancient knowledge are now being revealed, leaving us to question our past beliefs and perceptions. We also now have a much greater awareness of quantum physics, which allows us to perceive our reality in a new way, helping us to understand our own power to heal, our link to every living being and how we can create our own reality.

I feel like we live in quite a different time to the one I grew up in. Remaining in touch with your inner self and spirituality, feels more vital than ever. There are so many agendas and polarising views playing out in the world today, that staying true to ourselves is key without any judgment of others.

At this time, we are being regifted our forgotten and

hidden knowledge by indigenous cultures, but we forget that we were all once indigenous. I have a strong Celtic lineage on both sides of my family, and I can almost feel those ancestors calling me. I carry them in my DNA, after all, and they feel so close. I want to relearn what knowledge was denied and hidden from me. Sound healing and shamanism is the ancient path I travel to rediscover my roots.

What have you learned about your practical spirituality, and the human experience

Always listen to your intuition; you are the only one who truly knows what is right for you. Tuning into your higher self, whether that be through meditation, healing, quiet contemplation, spending time in nature, or whatever is best for you.

Ask spirit to help. You are not alone, and there is always help and guidance available. Often if I have a burning question, I will ask for guidance before bed. The answer to this will usually come to me in my dreams or by morning.

Maintain your boundaries. We are all on different paths, with different purposes, challenges and situations. Always do what is right for you, not because someone else told you to. Keep your vibration high and protect yourself from any energies or people that do not feel comfortable for you.

Always return to centre and ground. It is so easy to get swept up in our emotions and situations, but just remember that is just what they are, nothing else. Tune into your higher self; it will often give you a quite different perspective on a situation.

Never stop learning and growing. I think it is important to remember that the more you know, the less you know. Life is a continuous lesson, and I will never stop learning and growing.

Celebrate your life and that of others, be happy. We are so blessed to be living on this beautiful planet at this pivotal time in our history. We can make a difference.

4.10 Consciously manage your time: focus on activities and people that serve your purpose.

This section is about who you spend time with, and don't (including how to be alone). And it's about what you do, what you waste and how you find time for your spirituality. Jan shares her own early connection with spirituality, when divine support presented itself to support her through early childhood trauma. She reflects on how even some of the less positive personal interactions in her life served to strengthen her character, however uncomfortable they may have felt at the time.

4.10.1 Hang out with/talk with likeminded people

Spending time with people who are on the same wavelength is time when you are free to talk and act in line with yourself, and so is important for your mental and spiritual health and growth. This may not be your nearest family or your most established friends: thanks to the internet, we are able to join meet-up groups, workshops, courses, retreats or just social gatherings where it is possible to find people whom you connect with.

In the Western world, there is only a small percentage

of the population who believe and practise a non-religious spirituality based on some of the principles and paradigms mentioned in this book, so it's not surprising that people in this space might feel alone, especially at the beginning of their conscious journey. You are not. Check out the resources section in chapter five for more information about places to explore and ways to meet likeminded explorers. The Green Door Centre (formerly the Hamblin Centre) in particular, near Chichester in the UK, runs a number of events to facilitate great conversations and explorations. Check them out at thehamblinvision.org.uk (greendoorcentre.com).

4.10.2 Workshops and retreats

Attending workshops and retreats that interest you helps to raise your vibration because you are aligning with your passion, and this is accelerated by engaging with others with similar interests. If you have ever been in a workshop or at a concert full of people all aligned with the event, subject matter and each other, then you will know the energy can be electric. Everyone's focus helps to raise everyone else's vibration, which is also why group and global meditation can be very powerful.

There are many retreats and workshops available all over the world, so your choices will be influenced by your available time and finances and ability to travel. When I am surfing the internet for retreats and workshops, I always try to follow my gut feeling and ask myself the question 'does this align with my purpose?' I also sit with the question for a few days to see how and if it changes over time, and maybe discuss it with a trusted friend and ask for guidance through meditation. There are numerous techniques for asking your higher self or your guides a question. Meditation is a common means, but you can also use a pendulum (go to gaia.com for more information).

4.10.3 Others: managing your sharing

In leading a spiritual life, it is important to be conscious of the energy of others, as it may not be supportive of your own, or your growth. As a spiritual and awake person, you are more likely to be sensitive to other's energies and their intentions. It is my belief that approximately 95% of the Earth's population are not awake, so that's 7.2 billion people who will not resonate with most of this book. Put another way, that's 380 million people on Planet Earth, or only one in every twenty people you come across, who will resonate. Given the heavily controlled media, and given that acceptance of an alternative perspective of life and the existence of non-religious spirituality is growing only slowly, especially in Western environments, it is likely that most people you meet will be somewhere between sceptical to hostile if you discuss spiritual ideas, alternative accounts of human history, the notion of the life purpose and other themes set out in this book.

Humanity has a habit of rejecting that which it does not understand, and which 'groupthink', often led by the established powers of the time, has determined to not be okay. One of the best examples is the Catholic Church's 1633 prosecution of physicist and astronomer Galileo Galilei for holding the heretical belief that the Earth revolves around the sun. Of course, over time, this was globally accepted, but not before many individuals were persecuted for expressing it.

Not everyone is ready to have their paradigm shifted, so in order to maintain your focus on your purpose, vision and sanity, it is important to manage who you share your beliefs with. This theme appears often in writings dealing with the difficulty of leading an awake life in most societies. By contrast, there are still a few Amazonian peoples who remain connected with spirit in all aspects of their life, and thus their groupthink is quite different.

As mentioned earlier, it is important to connect with others on the same wavelength to give each other support in a safe space where you can be your true self. There are some that would argue that this approach is in some way defeatist. I would suggest that we must approach the outward projection of our inner beliefs in a way that is conscious, holds integrity for ourselves and allows us to sustain our practical spirituality in everyday life.

This is how we can manage the way we achieve our life purpose. For some, that is to be bold and vocal and public, but this is not appropriate for all. My personal journey to a position where I am ready to speak publicly and publish my beliefs on spirituality and the nature of human existence has taken over twenty years. But this is my journey. Others might reach the same position in more or less time and possibly in a different format. The important point is to take the route that is right for you.

Jan's Story

I liken my spiritual journey to *kintsugi*—the Japanese art of repairing the broken with pure gold. Now in my seventieth year, I look back and realise a major life-changing event took place in each and every one of my decades.

This started at the age of five, when I was struck down with polio and left unable to walk. I was thrown into eight years of a brutal medical regime, caregivers who gave no care, and separation from my parents for long periods of time. I took myself into a fantasy world of make believe—or was it actually a spiritual awakening that took me to a safe place? I believe it was, and that I have been revisiting that higher place ever since. When my parents were unable to visit due to the strict hospital rules, I was often aware of a presence and would sometimes feel as though someone was stroking me, even though I was alone. To this day, stroking is something I crave.

I have never sought a spiritual life. It has reached out to me and continues to do so. On occasions, I have felt separated from my spiritual self and I sought counselling to try and address my feelings of abandonment. When describing my memories of being in an isolation hospital, the counsellor remarked that 'I must have been terrified'. I thought about this for a while and then realised that, rather than terrified, I was defiant.

I recall one particular incident. I was nine and back in hospital for complicated, innovative surgery—a tendon transplant. It was lunchtime and despite being in a full leg plaster, the ward sister made me sit at the bench table. The lunch was mince. My lovely mum was a great cook, so I was unused to eating 'hospital dog food'. I refused to eat the mince. I was told I would sit there until I did. I was in pain. Blood was seeping through the plaster cast. All the other children ate the food out of fear and left the table. I remained. The mince became cold and covered in a thick layer of fat. Nurses told me that they could not throw it away because sister would see it was the only food in the bin. I sat there until tea time. Sister was convinced she would break me. She did not. How could she be scarier than polio? Defiance was born that day, and it never left. Angels surrounded me—I was safe in my own higher self.

I can recall many, many times reaching a point where I could see no happy outcome. Serious illness, bereavement, abandonment and isolation. Something would always happen to restore my joy. A sign I was being watched over, protected and supported. I would be driving and lost in negative thoughts. I would glance at the clock. 11.11—always 11.11—the sign of awakening and enlightenment. A gold thread running through my life. White feathers will always appear when I am seeking guidance. A message that love, peace, protection and light are around me.

Every aspect of my life has been affected by polio. The physical challenges, the ignorance, the pain. I do not see this as a negative, though. It has built my character. It has made me independent and resourceful. It also taught me how to look beyond the sepia aspects of life, to search for colour and to know that I am being watched over from a powerful higher realm.

4.11 Explore energy healing: learning to give and receive universal life force energy

In this section we explore the amazing world of energy healing. These are ancient healing techniques that can be traced back thousands of years and have the power to support all aspects of mental, pysicial and spiritual wellness and growth. Isabella shares with us her own spiritual life-path challenges and her strong connections with ancient healing modalities, which have practical benefits for her life today.

4.11.1 Energy healing

Energy healing is a holistic practice that activates the body's subtle energy systems to remove blocks. By breaking through these energetic blocks, the body's inherent ability to heal itself is stimulated.

As already mentioned, I believe the key to leading a more spiritually fulfilling life is connecting with the universal life force energy that exists all around us. There are multiple ways that this can be achieved, in terms of the places you visit, where you live and your spiritual practice, especially through meditation. Another important way is through energy healing, which could be self-healing and healing others. For thousands of years, humankind has used energy healing. This includes native cultures led by shamans and priests and priestesses, and those connected to the energy of existence and their surroundings, such as witches. These same types of people exist today, as do a multitude of others who practise and teach energy healing. These days, energy healing is sometimes referred to as complementary and holistic treatment and is often used alongside conventional medicine rather than precluding it.

One of the common principles of energy healing is to work with the chakras. The seven chakras, the energy transmission centres of the body, were first described in the Vedas. Reiki, the ancient tradition of energy healing, reintroduced through Japan in the early twentieth century, focuses on these centres. The discovery of meridians, the energy superhighways of the body, led traditional Chinese medicine practitioners to develop acupuncture. These ancient cultures used different modalities to stimulate the body's natural ability to heal, but they all recognise the power of internal energy.

Energy healing is based on scientific principles. All matter is made up of molecules. Even something that is solid, such as a table, is constantly vibrating. Humans, too, are vibrating. When you say someone has 'good vibes', you are really talking about that person's vibrational energy—and happy people tend to vibrate at a higher frequency. Places have vibes too. When you walk into a room in which a fight has just occurred, you may feel a dense energy that makes you want to leave right away. The beach has a light vibe due to the salt (a natural energy cleanser) and moving air. The air at the beach vibrates at a higher frequency as well.

4.11.2 Receiving energy healing

Anyone can benefit from energy healing. Just as you don't need to understand the law of gravity before you can fall down, you don't need to completely grasp the concept of energy healing before you dive into the practice. Any time is a good time to visit an energy healer, but it is important to try and go in with an open mind for maximum benefit. If you are stressed, anxious, or physically drained, an energy healing session can help you relax and feel more balanced. And if you're already feeling good, it's always possible to feel a little better.

You can maintain your energetic health at home. Just as you shower and brush your teeth every day, you should also be cleansing your energy regularly. Once you visit with an energy healer, keep the good vibes flowing by taking a bath in Epsom or pink Himalayan salts for twenty minutes whenever you start to feel the heaviness creeping back into your body. Smudging, or burning sage around you, can also help clear negativity from your energy field. Finally, high-vibe crystals can give your energy a little boost.

There are many types of energy healers, and each uses slightly different tools and techniques. You can find them practically everywhere. When you're looking for an energy healer, it's important to find one that you feel connected or called to. If you are new to energy healing, consider starting your search by dropping by a local yoga studio or asking a friend who's into alternative healing to get a referral to a reputable practitioner. There are many kinds of energy healing, and each calls on slightly different tools and techniques. The list below gives flavour of the different types that may be available.

Acupuncture

This is a system of medicine that has been practised in China and other countries for over 3,000 years. In Chinese medicine, life energy called chi (or qi) flows through the body via a network of subtle energy channels or meridians. Disease occurs when the flow becomes blocked, depleted, or out of balance. This can be caused by factors such as emotional stress, diet, overwork, infection, or injury.

Along each meridian are a number of acupuncture points at which the chi can be directly influenced. By inserting fine needles into these specific points, an acupuncturist can stimulate or sedate the flow of chi to rebalance the person's energy and thus remove the cause of disease.

Aromatherapy

Aromatherapy, sometimes called essential oil therapy, is an holistic healing treatment that uses natural plant extracts to promote health and well-being. The following guide to aromatherapy is provided by Emily Cronkleton and Debra

Rose Wilson's *Aromatherapy Uses and Benefits* (Cronkleton & Wilson, 2019).

The idea is to use essential oils to improve the health of body, mind and spirit. It enhances both physical and emotional health. Aromatherapy is thought of as an art and a science, and humans have used it for thousands of years. Ancient cultures in China, India, Egypt, South America and elsewhere incorporated aromatic plant components in resins, balms and oils that were used for medical and religious purposes.

Essential oil distillation is attributed to the Persians in the tenth century, although the practice may have been in use for a long time prior to this. French physicians in the nineteenth century recognised the potential of essential oils in treating disease. As medical doctors became more established in the nineteenth century, they focused on the development of chemical drugs, however, some French and German doctors recognised the role of natural botanicals in treating illness. The term 'aromatherapy' was coined by French perfumer and chemist René-Maurice Gattefossé (Gattefosse, 1937). He had previously discovered the healing potential of lavender in treating burns. The book discusses the use of essential oils in treating medical conditions.

Aromatherapy works through the sense of smell and skin absorption using products such as:

- Diffusers
- Aromatic spritzers
- Inhalers
- Bath salts
- Body oils, creams, or lotions for massage or topical application
- Facial steamers

- Hot and cold compresses
- Clay masks

You can use these alone or in any combination. There are nearly a hundred types of essential oils available and generally, people use the most popular. Essential oils are available online, in health food stores and in some regular supermarkets. It's important to buy from a reputable producer, especially since regulation of oils differs across the world. This ensures you're buying a quality product that is 100 per cent natural and does not contain any additives or synthetic ingredients.

Each essential oil has an array of unique healing properties, uses, and effects. Combining essential oils to create a synergistic blend creates even more benefits. Aromatherapy can be used to:

- Manage pain
- Improve sleep quality
- Reduce stress, agitation and anxiety
- Soothe sore joints
- Treat headaches and migraines
- Alleviate side effects of chemotherapy
- Ease discomforts of labour
- Fight bacteria, virus, or fungus
- Improve digestion
- Improve hospice and palliative care
- Boost immunity

Some of the most commonly used essential oils are given below (Lin, 2021). Always seek qualified and approved medical advice when using treatments on yourself and others.

- Lavender oil reducea stress, pain and improves sleep
- Tea tree oil is an antiseptic, antimicrobial or antifungal. Can help with acne, athlete's foot and ringworms.

- Frankincense oil is an anti-inflammatory and improves mood and sleep. May improve asthma and might prevent gum disease.
- Peppermint oil has anti-inflammatory, antifungal and antimicrobial properties, eases headaches, fights fatigue, lifts mood, reduces gut spasms, supports digestion and memory, settles stomachs and reduces the impact of irritable bowel syndrome and gastric irritation.
- Eucalyptus oil soothes a stuffed-up nose, relieves pain, fights against the herpes simplex virus.
- Lemon oil reduces anxiety and depression, eases nausea, kills bacteria and may improve cognitive functions of people with Alzheimer's.
- Lemongrass oil relieves stress, anxiety and depression, heals wounds, kills bacteria, prevents the growth of the fungus found in athlete's foot, ringworm and jock itch. May reduce blood sugar in those with type-two diabetes.
- Orange oil kills bacteria, reduces anxiety and pain.
- Rosemary oil improves brain function, promotes hair growth, reduces pain and stress, lifts mood and reduces joint inflammation. If you're pregnant or have epilepsy or high blood pressure, it's advised to avoid using rosemary oil. (Lin, 2021)
- Bergamot oil reduces anxiety, lifts mood, lowers blood pressure.
- Cedarwood oil helps with sleep and anxiety.

Bowen technique

This facilitates deep healing both physically and emotionally. The gentle Bowen moves aim to calm your nervous system, enabling your body to engage with its own healing abilities more effectively, relieving tension and strain and assisting you to return to a more balanced way of being

Crystal healing

The aim is to treat the whole person and to bring balance within the individual's subtle energies. The client's body is gently reminded of its own connection to nature and spirit ('all that is'). By reinstating this connection and using other powerful crystal healing techniques, a natural recalibration often occurs that brings with it the benefits of conscious health and wellbeing. The use of crystals is personal and can be complex, as so many are available. It is important to do your research and to 'feel' the energy of crystals before you acquire them. Below is a taster of options and their suggested uses, with reference to reiki healing, but the general theme is consistent. (Cuts, 2022):

- Clear quartz: used to balance the entire auric field
- Amethyst: for balancing and opening the crown chakra and third eye chakra
- Citrine: used to balance the solar plexus chakra and to bring joy into the energy system
- Rose quartz: used to support the heart chakra.
- Red jasper: balances the root chakra
- Bloodstone: provides grounding energy and balances the root and heart chakras
- Sodalite: supports the throat chakra
- Carnelian: used to balance the sacral chakra
- Aquamarine: used to bring a sense of calm to the body, mind and spirit
- Smoky quartz: provides uplifting and cleansing energy to the chakras.

Please do your own research and find crystals that 'feel' right for you.

EFT (Emotional Freedom Technique)

This incorporates theories from holistic therapies such as acupressure, energy medicine and neuro-linguistic programming. Many eastern medicine models are founded on the belief that there are channels of energy within the body. It is thought that when these channels (known as meridians) become blocked, energy becomes unbalanced. When this happens, it is thought to lead to physical and emotional symptoms.

In the Western world, we are beginning to catch up with the premise that emotional health is imperative to physical health. As well as affecting our wellbeing, emotional blocks can lead to limiting beliefs and behaviours, which may result in phobias, anxiety, depression, or even addiction. EFT acknowledges this and combines energy medicine with psychological interventions for a truly holistic approach to health.

In a similar way to acupuncture, EFT looks to release blocked energy by stimulating the meridian points. Rather than using needles however, this therapy uses tapping techniques.

Tapping (using the fingertips) on certain points on the body, combined with voicing positive affirmations is thought to neutralise the emotional block in energy.

Flower essences

Flower therapy, or essence therapy, is a form of complementary and alternative medicine. It's based on the idea that flowers have a healing vibrational energy (Nunez & Fontane, 2020). The practice uses flower essences, which are liquids infused with a flower's energy. They're also called flower remedies. They're believed to improve negative thoughts and emotions.

Some studies say they can ease anxiety and pain, but more research is needed. There's usually no harm in using them, but most do have a tiny amount of alcohol. Use an alcohol-free version if you're pregnant or breastfeeding.

Modern flower essences were created by Edward Bach, a British physician, in the 1930s. According to Bach, the energy of flowers can balance your emotions. He believed this can bring about mental, physical and spiritual wellness. Today, people use flower essences for the same purpose. You can buy them in stores or get them from an essence therapist. There is some evidence flower remedies may help anxiety and pain. They're also believed to improve immunity, depression, and various psychological disorders, but the science is lacking.

Flower essences are made in the following way:

- Flowers are submerged in natural spring water
- The water is boiled or placed in the sun (allegedly, sun exposure helps extract the energy of flowers)
- The water is filtered and preserved with brandy. The finished essence contains no part of the flower.

Essences can be made with non-flowering plants and crystals using the same method. They can also be made without alcohol (Nunez & Fontane, 2020).

Homeopathy

As one of the most widely used systems of medicine in the world, homeopathy is a fascinating, versatile and truly holistic way of working with people of all ages to overcome or cope with many health issues, be they physical, mental or emotional. Homeopathy involves giving the patient highly diluted substances, called remedies, mainly in tablet form, with the aim of gently triggering the body's innate power to heal.

Each of us will experience our illness or health issue in our own way, so care and time need to be taken during the initial consultation to gather as much information as possible about you and your unique symptoms to build up a detailed understanding of who you are, your general energy level, your past medical history, your way of life, and details of any other complaints and how you experience them. A homeopathic Remedy or group of remedies is then selected to suit your person as a whole, mind and body.

Hopi ear-candling

Also known as 'thermal auricular therapy', this originated from a native American tribe called the Hopis (the name means 'peaceful people'). It is a pleasant and non-invasive treatment of the ears, and is used to treat a variety of conditions including the effects of colds, ear-wax build up and sinus stress. Treatments can also involve face, head, neck and shoulder massage.

Hot stone massage

Hot stone massage is a speciality treatment that can work much deeper than a traditional massage. It uses smooth heated basalt stones (volcanic stones known for their heat retaining qualities) as part of the massage. They can act as an extension of the therapist's hands and, when placed on specific points on the body, can improve the flow of energy.

Hypnotherapy and neuro-linguistic programming

Hypnosis is a natural state of deep relaxation and concentration with heightened awareness. You are not asleep, nor is there any possibility you will lose control of yourself. It uses the subconscious to enhance the power of the mind to aid the improvement of both your physical and mental health. Hypnotherapy and Neuro Linguistic Programming (NLP) help to break unhelpful thinking patterns and create new positive thoughts which in turn make you change. You cannot be made to do anything you do not want to do while under hypnosis, but you can actively help yourself deal with the challenges of life.

The benefits of hypnotherapy are a deeply relaxing and calming experience, helping the mind and body move forward. Relaxation, both physically and mentally, helps balance the body. Using NLP and the solution-focused approach, we can bring about change for the better—fast!

Indian head massage

Deeply calming and relaxing, this is an ancient therapeutic treatment that has been practised in India for more than a thousand years. It combines a range of massage techniques with gentle stretches to loosen and mobilise the muscles and joints of the upper back, shoulders, upper arms, neck, scalp, ears and face. As you are seated for this therapy, it is ideal for situations where it may not be appropriate to give a fully body massage. It is also a good introduction to massage.

Integrated energy therapy

This is a safe, gentle, nurturing way to empower and balance your life by helping to release patterns of the past for good. IET uses a unique cellular memory map to target specific areas in the body where these cellular memories are stored, helping to release them on all levels—physical, emotional, mental, and spiritual. It is based on the belief that negative or traumatic experiences, stress, unexpressed emotions, fear, anger, resentment or self-limiting beliefs are stored in the cells of the body much as facts are stored in the cells of the brain. If not cleared from our system, they disrupt the flow of vital life force and may cause unrest, chronic pain, dis-ease, sadness, or depression.

Kinesiology

This was created in the 1960s by American chiropractor George Goodheart. He discovered that each muscle is related to an energy circuit and each circuit is connected to an organ, a gland, a meridian and an emotion. If there is stress in the circuit, it becomes blocked or thrown out of balance. Kinesiology uses the action of muscle testing to access the subconscious mind, and it corrects imbalances of energy within the physical, emotional and mental systems of the body.

Emotions can cause stress, whether it be anxiety, sadness, depression, grief, fear, and so on. Stress causes cortisol production, which can then crystallise in organs and create imbalances in the body. If emotions are left unresolved, they can start blocking up, causing physical issues. Remove the root cause of the problem and everything can flow again.

Massage

Massage is the manipulation of the body's soft tissues and is an energy healing practice. It releases tension in the muscles, encourages the flow of lymph and allows for deep relaxation. Archaeological evidence of massage has been found in many ancient civilizations, including China, India, Japan, Korea, Egypt, Rome, Greece and Mesopotamia, as far back as 4300 BP. Massage techniques are commonly applied with hands, fingers, elbows, knees, forearms, feet, or a device. The purpose is generally to treat bodily stress or pain. There are many different types of massage, including (but not limited to): deep tissue, manual lymphatic drainage, medical, sports, structural integration, Swedish, Thai, trigger point and tantric.

The myriad massaging techniques available mean that most people are able to see a massage therapist for their specific needs, including purely for relaxation. It is worth taking the time to research what is being offered to find the right therapy and therapist for your needs.

Medium/psychic readings

Mediumship is the ability to communicate with people in spirit. Using a guide, mediums hear or see images, or otherwise sense the consciousness of those who are no longer with us. Messages can be relayed to those who want guidance or comfort from their loved ones. However, please note that messages cannot be guaranteed.

Nutritional therapy

This aims to assess the biochemical and physiological processes occurring in an individual and identify where imbalances may be causing or contributing to health problems. Nutritional therapy uses an evidence-based, holistic approach in its assessment and management of a client's symptoms in order to facilitate and enhance the body's ability to heal itself through nutrition and lifestyle changes. Each person is seen as unique and therefore nutrition plans are bespoke.

Reconnective healing

Reconnective Healing is a return to an optimal state of balance. It is the result of interacting with the comprehensive spectrum of frequencies that consist of energy, light and information. This healing transcends traditional energy healing techniques as it is neither a therapy nor a treatment; it does not focus on symptoms, diagnose or treat. We simply interact with the frequencies, restoring balance in the body and bringing about effects that are often instantaneous and tend to be lifelong.

When reconnective healing frequencies entrain with our energy body, we emit and vibrate at a higher level of light. This has been shown to restructure our DNA, resulting in the emission of measurably higher levels of bio-photonics. Stanford Professor Emeritus Dr William Tiller says that when information carried through the reconnective healing frequencies is introduced, it creates coherence and order. In other words, greater harmony and balance within us.

Reflexology

Reflexology is a complementary therapy that works on the feet or hands enabling the body to heal itself. Following illness, stress or injury, the body is in a state of imbalance and vital energy pathways are blocked, preventing the body from functioning effectively. Reflexology can be used to restore and maintain the body's natural equilibrium and therefore encourage healing.

Reiki healing

Reiki is a natural healing method that uses the universal life energy, or chi, to stimulate the body's healing processes and promote balance, health and harmony. Non-intrusive and gentle, it has also been called therapeutic touch or laying-on-of-hands. Many people credit reiki with accelerating their healing, although it makes no claims to cure. Reiki is simply energy that works by harmonising and balancing the chakras.

Shiatsu

Shiatsu is a nurturing full-body massage based on the principles of Chinese medicine. It is deeply relaxing and helps releases muscular and emotional tensions and strengthens areas of weakness. It is also beneficial for pregnant women and new mothers.

Sound healing

Sound healing uses the principles of vibration and resonance as a form of deep healing. Records of sound healing date back to ancient Egypt and Greece. It can be thought of as part meditation, part listening. This process takes you on an inner journey of relaxation. It can help to restore and rebalance, enabling inner stillness, total relaxation with potential for deep healing. Find out more from Estelle at www.thelondonsoundhealer.co.uk.

Thai yoga massage

Many of the techniques in Thai massage seem to be common sense, and in Thailand, rural workers have for generations exchanged massage with family members. In tandem, there is a more scientific form based on yoga theory that was introduced to Thailand some 2,000 years ago. Using stretching and acupressure techniques, its aim is to aid the flow of energy around the body to restore balance in much the same way as yoga.

In more recent years, the theory of Thai massage has been borne out by research into the fascial 'net' that allows body-wide connections between muscles and are used in osteopathy and myofascial release. By a process of unravelling, the therapist can release tension and encourage healthy patterns of movement. The treatment is suitable for all body types, irrespective of flexibility. It is particularly effective for pregnant women.

Therapeutic touch

This involves the therapist placing their hands on or near their patient's body with the intention to help or heal. In doing so, therapists believe they are consciously directing or modulating an individual's energies by interacting with their energy field. The focus is on balancing the energies of the total person and stimulating the body's natural healing ability rather than on the treatment of specific physical diseases (Bakken, 2016).

Therapeutic touch is based on the following assumptions:

- The human being is an open energy system composed of layers of energy that are in constant interaction with self, others and the environment
- Illness is an imbalance in an individual's energy field
- Clearing or balancing the energy field promotes health
- All humans have natural abilities to heal and enhance healing in others.

Therapeutic touch defined as a specific energy technique was developed by Delores Krieger, whereas healing touch is a collection of techniques developed and compiled by Janet Mentgen in the early 1980s (Bakken, 2016).

A more physical definition of therapeutic touch is that it is a treatment that involves the therapist touching the patient in a specific way. Broadly defined as the manual manipulation of muscles and soft tissue in the body, massage is a form of touch therapy, as is craniofacial massage. Any kind of touch, stimulates the vagus nerve, which has branches running throughout the body. It regulates the functioning of internal organs and counteracts your fight/flight system. Four chemicals have been shown to change with physical touch. The hormone oxytocin increases, and this has been shown to lower stress and anxiety; the body's feel-good neurotransmitters serotonin and dopamine also rise and cortisol levels decrease, which can lower blood pressure and heart rate.

4.11.3 Giving energy healing

Any activity that raises your personal energy vibration and expands your consciousness is a positive from a practical spirituality perspective, and giving energy healing is definitely that. All human beings have the ability to do this for the benefit of themselves and others. For some it is part of their purpose and path to offer this to the rest of humanity in this lifetime. If you feel the desire to explore this, then you should.

An introduction to most modalities is usually fairly easily to access. For example, reiki can provide a quick platform from which to start and to see results fairly quickly, if that is an important motivator for you. As you research, you will no doubt come across a wide variety of prices and scopes on offer. Where courses and training appear to be excessively priced, to provide a step up for something that we are all inherently programmed to do, then you have a choice about the value you feel you are getting from all of the other aspects of the offer, for example, the timing, location, post-course support and practice opportunities, as well as the experience of the instructor, the depth of guidance and the handout materials.

If you are not sure which energy healing modality to try, you should sample a few, both as a receiver and as a giver. Often there are opportunities to join others to share a healing exchange, for example with reiki shares and massage exchanges. These events are usually at minimal cost. As you try out different modalities, remember that the act of giving through energy healing should feel good, like a passion and an honour rather than a chore or the 'day job'. If you have escaped your unhappy corporate life to end up feeling stuck again giving energy healing, you are probably still on your journey to find your purpose and true alignment.

Isabella's story

Describe your spirituality

I believe our soul has chosen when to incarnate, which body, which era and which parents. This is to evolve from our last soul's journey, to complete any missions that we didn't overcome in our last incarnation and be more evolved for our next life path. The more awakened and more connected to spirit we are, the more we will turn into source energy.

What is your earliest memory of spiritual awakening?

My earliest memory was seeing spirits when I was around eleven years old. I grew up around crystals and oracle cards, so my family supported me in my gifts. I started meditating and connecting to Buddhism when I was nineteen to help me cope with depression and eating disorders. This was my first step in the door. I received reiki when I was twenty-five and from then on knew that was what I wanted to do; until then, I had felt lost, with no sense of purpose. That grew into crystal healing and tapping into strong psychic abilities.

How did you feel? What challenges did you face?

I felt very excited; it felt like home. It triggered many awakenings to a healthier lifestyle, going vegan for example—but it also made me aware that I was in relationships that were no longer aligned with me, be it in friends, family or love. That part of letting go was tough; I was with my partner for three years and we were planning on spending the rest of our lives together. But once the transition started, I felt as if I was born again. It was and is true alignment: challenges arise and my human self doesn't want to let go, but I know it is for the highest purpose and the level of growth is massive. My family was very supportive and I eventually found a community where talking about inner child healing is as normal as what used to be my 'how are you?'

What happened next? What did you do next after your awakening?

I started practising daily meditation, mindfulness when cooking, doing readings for friends and family, wearing and carrying crystals, practising self-reiki, journaling and connecting in a way that helped me to receive messages from consciousness. For me, this was partly due to me Celtic roots, the fae woodland realms that I connected with through past-life regression. I am grateful that I am able to go into my past lives very easily, so this knowledge comes quickly. Over the years I connected with Quan Yin, Rose Lineage, Merlin, dragons, Excalibur, Buddha, Brigid, Morrigan, Ganesh and Kali, amongst other personal guides. It has been a process of step-by-step moving and shedding old skin, overcoming fear and stepping into my light.

A key moment?

The earliest was moving to the UK when I was nine, when I started to see spirits and use angel cards. As I said, I reached one the lowest periods in my life at nineteen, suffering from bulimia and self-harm, and this is when I connected to Buddhism. I started to reach a higher level of consciousness through transcendental meditation at twenty-three; this was the first moment I began to connect to my dharma.

Two years later, it hit home after I received my first reiki session. The downloads and awareness were so huge it felt like spirit was shaking me, saying WAKE UP, THIS IS YOUR PATH. That took me to completing my master's course in both reiki and crystal healing. The energy I receive from crystals is like nothing else on this planet. Since 2019, the journey has felt like a never-ending one, and the break-up with my partner was a pivotal moment. Receiving attunements from reiki masters, having the confidence to teach crystal healing, the move to London and now being in community with like-minded people is like nothing I have felt before. My growth has been immense and I am so proud of myself. I am currently doing a course on integrating your light and dark masculine energies, which has already brought up a lot of lightbulb moments. Next month I start my shamanic training—my zest for life is immense!

What does your spiritual day/week look like now?

I meditate, chant, dance, sing and read daily. Even if it

is just five minutes. My diet is vegan and I have never felt so connected to source. My moon time is extremely important to me now and I rest during it; I sit and see what has come up during the cycle that I want to release. I collect my blood and release her at a stream in a forest. If you bleed, I urge you to do the same. Connection to womb wisdom is so important. I hold by monthly retreats and facilitate monthly women's circles. I continue learning through whatever is coming up in daily interactions, seeing people as mirrors for myself and my actions. Integrating shadow work, inner child healing as well as working with feminine and masculine energy. I use my social media platform to give free card readings for the collective and I have paying clients for in-depth readings, reiki and crystal healing.

And how do you feel now?

Alive. Connected. I used to feel lost; I now know my dharma. Being surrounded by people who do the same work—it is not a nine-to-five, it's a way of life. As Ghandi said, when death comes, I will be ready 'ram, ram'.

What have you learned about your practical spirituality and the human experience?

I have learned that a lot of us are in misalignment, whether it is the food we eat or the numbing TV we watch. We often play the victim, but if we all connect to our innate power, we will see that we are all consciousness: I am you and you are me, so therefore why would I want to harm myself? Of course, there are the factors of race, sex and sexuality, but if we were all connected, we would see the pain in everyone and allow ourselves to feel and be compassionate.

4.12 Visit special 'energy places'

Our final set of tools focuses on the importance and value of visiting special places on our amazing Planet Earth, which is, of course, a living organism too. . There is an established and ancient history to support the idea that energy flows through it, towards it and from it. Those flows, and their interactions with the cosmos and existence itself, lead to places on Earth that hold special meaning and purpose, with which we can engage on a physical and spiritual level. Elijah Otim shares with us some of his interesting experiences over the years from visiting special energy places. But first, a short history of the notion of Mother Earth/Pacha Mama.

4.12.1 Mother Earth/Gaia/Pacha Mama: her history and importance—in brief

Quite simply, Mother Earth or Gaia, is life (Gaia, 2017). She is all, the very soul of the Earth. She is a goddess who, by all accounts, inhabits the planet, offering life and nourishment to her children. In the ancient civilizations, she was revered as mother, nurturer and giver of life. She goes by many names: Gaia (from Greek mythology), Pacha Mama (from the Incas), Bhudevi, Prithivi, Vasundhara or Vasudha (from the Vedas), Unci Maka (from Native American traditions), as well as Ancestral Mother, Mother Earth and Primordial Goddess.

Every culture has their version of the Earth goddess. In some cases, she predates writing: pre-linguistic references to her have been found, alongside shrines, statues and paintings, in every corner of the globe. She is the first goddess, the primeval one, the creator of all life and the fullness of her legacy is still being resurrected after patriarchal suppression. To the Greeks, Gaia was the goddess of raw, maternal power. In the beginning, there was a chaos of nebulous ethers waiting to take form. This primordial landscape awaited direction; it was then that the spirit of Gaia arrived to give structure to the formless and the Earth was conceived.

She became the Earth, birthing all form of landscape, plant and creature. Although her creation was majestic, her solitude was great. She longed for love and created the sky with whom she mated, igniting a creative force that birthed countless offspring: time and the Fates, the Muses and the oceans, to name a few. She's considered the primeval mother, from whom all gods—and life itself—descended.

As the prevalence of gods and goddesses in the nineteenth and twentieth centuries faded away, so did history books' tales of female pharaohs, women scientists and Amazon warriors. History is written by the victors—and the victors are most often men. This left a void in our collective consciousness and Gaia was relegated to mythology alone. With the emergence of feminism in the 1970s, all that changed, and a groundbreaking pro-female establishment was founded, providing a new understanding of how our planet operates.

In 1970, chemist James Lovelock and his research partner Lynn Margulis (the wife of Carl Sagan at the time) proposed that the earth is a living being, self-regulating the elements that sustain life on it. This revolutionary hypothesis was seen as heretical, but has since been accepted as a theory, rather than a mere hypothesis. Their work suggested chemicals 'talk' to one another, that all elements work in harmony to ensure the biosphere is sustained. The stability of life and the consistent ability of the planet to self-regulate and protect its creatures connotes a universe more intelligent than previously imagined.

Far beyond the mythological Gaia, the name has come to represent an all-loving, nurturing and intelligent cosmic force that oversees life on Earth. Those who research the goddess traditions have worked tirelessly to resurrect the ancient teachings of the Great Mother and re-establish her presence as a force of love. More than saving the planet or participating in Earth Day celebrations, we can treat every day like a ceremony. To be in a sincere connected relationship with Gaia, we must acknowledge her sundry gifts and be open to receive her wisdom.

4.12.2 Interactions with special energy points

As we have established, Planet Earth is a living organism. The true nature and absolute depth of knowledge of how energy flows around and through the Earth remains a work in progress, but it is known that in certain places, flows can be detected by humans and sometimes by technology, and these can be extreme. These special places, which allow humans to connect to the divine source, have been known for thousands of years. It is believed some of the most ancient structures and places of worship on Earth were located and built to align and connect with the special energy in those locations, for example, Stonehenge, Avebury and Glastonbury in the UK, the Great Pyramid and similar structures on the Giza Plateau in Egypt, Mount Shasta and Sedona in North America, and many more. See chapter six for a list of special places to visit.

Elijah Otim's story

Experiencing special energy places

Stonehenge and Avebury, UK

I have been visiting special energy places for over thirty years. As I grew up in the UK, the most obvious place was Stonehenge, which I visited in the early 1990s. In those days, you could hire the whole site for a few hours, which is what a few of us did one Friday night. This allowed us to meditate within and touch the stones, which even then was not easy for the public to do, in terms of access. So, touching the stones as part of meditation was my first experience of feeling very powerful jolts of energy coming into my body , through my hands from a natural source. The experience was almost addictive and was certainly paradigm-shifting for me.

Around the same time, I visited the ancient set of stone circles with the village of Avebury inside them. The energy experience here was not as extreme as my first visit to Stonehenge, but there was certainly a sense of a powerful and ancient presence there. I visit Avebury fairly regularly, and often spend time in the church. It is a place of recharge and reconnection for me, and there is a particular stone, to the north of the village, that I am drawn to, and that I have received messages through or from whilst there.

Glastonbury Tor

My first visit to Glastonbury Tor and town (which is not to be confused with the music festival), was in 2019. I have visited at least four times each year since. It has become a recharging and grounding location for me in this life. I feel very at home when I am there. The location is considered the Heart Chakra of Planet Earth, and is also know as the Avalon of Arthurian legend. It is a special and powerful place, and for those open and sensitive to energies, it can be a challenging place. On my various trips, through meditation and just presence in the environment, I have received poignant messages related to questions that I needed to resolve at the time. I have been aware of the presence of spirits, including faeries, and once on an equinox visit with a shaman friend of mine, we both saw the clouds moving in front of the Moon, in a staccato motion, not smooth as you would normally expect. I have no idea what caused this. It's a great example of a real experience that has the capacity to expand your consciousness. Check out the Camelot Retreat Centre for a place to stay in Glastonbury (www.camelotretreat.com). There is a very large crystal placed over the vortex in the middle of the property. It's a great place to meditate and meet other fellow spiritual explorers visiting the town.

On one visit I climbed up to the tor around midnight to meditate. I was alone in the building up there, but struggling with my meditation—there was too much mind going on, and I was getting frustrated by my apparent lack of progress. After about fifteen minutes, two young guys appeared, very loud, high on magic mushrooms, talking incessantly and unable to sit still and trying to engage with me. Their performamce was nothing short of comical and once I had decided they were harmless, I surrended to this strange turn of events. They departed as swiftly as they had arrived, and left me chuckling to myself about divine intervention, and that sometimes the universe and its guides will intervene, just to make you smile and laugh and remind you not to take life too seriously all the time! Thank you …

Bell Rock, Sedona, Arizona

Sedona is a special ancient place, and is said to hold a number of interdimensional vortices in its surrounds. I was drawn to visit the location twice in 2017. On my first trip I was climbing Bell Rock, one of the significant vortex sites. I found myself struggling with the route I had chosen to reach the top, where a specific location was said to hold the vortex. Feeling under some stress, I lowered myself down and found a ledge to rest on and lie down. I felt overcome by energy and emotion whilst there, and at one point I tried to get up, but a voice instructed me to stay where I was. There was no one else nearby, that I could see. After a while I was able to get up, and realised I was actually about 10 yards from the location I had been looking for. Frustratingly, I don't usually remember my dreams, but that night I had a very clear dream where I was talking to myself, or rather a version of a future self was telling me to stop messing about and get on with my purpose. At that stage I was still working that out, but I guess he was giving me a nudge! Thank you …

5: Resources to keep learning and growing

THIS BOOK was written to create a guide for specific techniques and a path to other sources of knowledge. Humanity's creation of wisdom dates back thousands of years, through stories and songs in the written and oral traditions, and in more recent times, through film. Today, most of us have access to inspirational speakers from all over the world and, through the internet, a platform to speak ourselves and be listened to by those who resonate with the message.

By seeking out areas of interest and being aware of signs that point us in certain directions, particularly those that align with our purposes, we continually raise our vibration and grow, even if we are not fully conscious of it. Often, new knowledge that we are drawn to explore may appear misaligned with our core values, but we should reflect on the differences and decide how we feel about it, even if it is to discard it as something we do not resonate with. This pause is important, because it strengthens our alignment with that which we do resonate with.

This section of the book lists a number of the resources I have used over the past thirty years, and includes books, events, workshops and films. Each of these appeared in my life as they needed to and resonated with me. Often in bookshops I would—and still do—just ground myself and wander around until a title jumps out at me. Invariably, whatever it is, I buy it. Internet book shopping is different, but perhaps a similar principle can be adopted as you browse through book lists. I believe it is important continually to look for your opportunities for growth. Keep visiting bookshops and fairs and putting yourself in a place where the opportunity to learn and grow is prevalent.

5.1 External support groups

There are multiple sources of group activity available to connect with likeminded people on their path, and explore spiritual pursuits. This might be part of online groups, face-to-face groups, meditation groups, spiritual philosophy groups, walking groups and even wild swimming groups.

From my experience, there are many opportunities out there and Facebook is a good place to start looking for them. Meet-ups are another possibility. The word 'spirituality' and it's use is broad, so it may take a while to find a group whose energy you gel with, but give it time and effort, and try to connect with your gut feelings to determine what resonates with you.

5.2 Spiritual life coaching

As a spiritual life coach, I am here to help you develop your journey within the practicalities of daily life. My approach is based on personal experience accrued from years of living with the frustration of trying to combine my challenging professional careers and my family responsibilities with a burning desire to explore my spiritual journey, develop my spiritual practice and ultimately discover and live my life purpose.

My experience as a reiki master energy healer and my training in neuro-linguistic programming and life coaching with Tony Robbins provides a framework to draw on my fifty years of life experience to help you understand the roots of your 'perceived blockages' and develop strategies to move yourself in the direction of your choosing, towards achieving the fulfilment you desire.

I am based on the south coast of the UK, for in-person sessions, and also available online via Zoom and Skype. If you would like to know more, and to discuss how I could help you, then please get in touch to arrange a complementary clarity session where we can explore your aspirations and desires for your life and spiritual journey.

5.3 Courses and training

5.3.1 Mindfulness and spirituality

- Michael Beckwith (www.michaelbeckwith.com)
- The Green Door Centre (formally The Hamblin Centre) West Sussex (www.greendoorcentre.com)
- Hamblin Vision (www.thehamblinvision.org.uk)
- Mind Valley (www.mindvalley.com)

5.3.2 Reiki energy healing

- Anthony Oyo, UK (www.consciousnessawaken.org)
- Michael Kauffman Reiki Training and Meditation (www.reiki-meditation.co.uk)

5.3.3 Life coaching

- Spiritual Life Coaching, Anthony Oyo (www.consciousnessawaken.org)
- Jack Canfield (www.jackcanfield.com)

- Neuro-linguistic programming, NLP World (UK) (www.nlpworld.co.uk)
- Tony Robbins Life Coaching (rmtcenter.com)

6: Special places to visit

ALL PLACES listed below are special because they allow we humans to connect with the natural and special energy that facilitates a more direct connection with the divine source. This is important and useful for our growth because it enables a more efficient, higher vibrational connection that might be important for our purpose, or simply for grounding us and allowing a 'calming down' from all the 'noise' of life. Of course, there is also the opportunity to access the wisdom that may be necessary for your life purpose.

6.1 Types of special places

I have divided the following catalogue of special places in my own way, but there maybe other categorisations that are more relevant to you. Either way, it's important to take action ... so go visit, connect and enjoy.

6.1.1 Ancient sites

Ancient peoples were far more connected than we are to Mother Earth, spirit, nature, animals, the environment, the cosmos, time, space and the natural flow of energy throughout the planet. It is important to note that this knowledge still exists in the cultures of natives peoples in certain parts of the world, in particular the Amazon rainforest and amongst Australian first nation peoples. Ancient sites such as Stonehenge, Glastonbury and Avebury were built where they were for reasons that reflect their builders' connection with energy, spirit and the higher source.

6.1.2 Ancient and remote woodlands

There are ancient woodlands all over the world. There are parts of the Amazon that remain unexplored, even today. But even in Europe there are swaths of woodlands that have escaped human development. These locations are likely to hold the energy and memory of human engagement, and if inhabited by ancient peoples they will be imbued with traces of spiritual ceremonies and connections and inherent special energy, collected before that engagement. In the UK, close to the South Downs Way, near Chichester, there is an ancient woodland known as Kingley Vale that is considered to be one of Europe's most impressive yew forests, with trees that are as much as 2,000 years old—making them some of the oldest organisms in Great Britain. It has a rich and diverse heritage, with remains of a Romano-Celtic temple at Bow Hill, an Iron Age settlement site known as Goosehill Camp, the Devil's Humps barrows from the Bronze Age and prehistoric flint mines. There are also a number of unidentified archaeological remains in the form of linear earthworks, a rectangular enclosure known as Bow Hill Camp and evidence of settlement at the base of the hill.

6.1.3 Thermal healing sites

Across the world, thermal spas have enjoyed a reputation for healing over many centuries. They have long been believed to have the power to treat a range of ailments, as well as helping to maintain good health in general.

Thermal springs occur naturally all over the world where water rises to the surface after being heated by volcanic activity. Many ancient civilisations, such as the Greeks and Romans, built baths at the site of the spring to take advantage of this natural phenomenon. The popularity of thermal spas sprang from the belief that they could cure many ailments and in general were good for people's health.

Although the science behind the effectiveness of thermal baths is unclear, the waters continue to attract visitors who swear by their beneficial properties. One reason for the healing power of the waters may be their high mineral content. This differs according to the rock and soil found at each spa, but the minerals absorbed by the body when bathing are thought to help with many ailments and illnesses.

The temperature of the water is also thought to aid the body's healing process by relaxing and soothing joints and muscles and encouraging the body to purify itself of toxins by sweating them out through the skin. Whatever the reason for their healing powers, spend time in a thermal spa and your body will thank you for it.

In addition to the physical benefits of spas, this extended period in a hot pool is also a great example of 'soul care', according to Keri Wyatt Kent, author of *GodSpace: Embracing the Inconvenient Adventure of Intimacy with God* (Kent, 2017). She writes: 'Our weary souls need time to be still, time to just rest. When we make that time, we can hear the voice that tells us that we are beloved, that grace can't be earned—it's just a gift. So many of us feel we're running on empty, and we long for replenishment. Think about energy as water in a cup. We pour out for everyone else, and we're always running. Our souls are jumpy. The water is sloshed out, given away, depleted. In order to refill a cup, you've got to hold it still. We pray "God fill me up", but we don't hold still long enough (physically or emotionally) to let God pour that peace, joy and energy into our souls. A hot thermal bath experience can give us that space.'

It is my belief that thermal baths allow us to enter a more meditative state, where we can feel relaxation and increased connection with the source. I am convinced the energy associated with water flow and its rising and heating from the depths of the earth—from Gaia—must also provide an opportunity to access higher vibrational energies.

6.1.4 Ley lines

Ley lines, or the Earth's energy grid, have been described in various ways. The TV broadcast *Earth's Energy Grid* (Kanaga, 2016) suggests that 'just as we have our own energy centres or chakras, Mother Earth also has hers' and we are 'connected to the Earth through the subtle electrical current that runs around the entire planet. These electrical currents are known as "ley lines" and are almost like Mother Earth's veins.' The programme goes on to suggest that they are 'lines of energy that coil around the earth in a similar fashion as a strand of DNA, and that vertices where the lines intersect are believed to be high points of energy, or to have high concentrations of electrical charge'.

Recent studies have shown the existence of ancient and sacred structures located on straight-line alignments across the planet, including the Egyptian pyramids, Machu Picchu, Stonehenge and Angkor Wat. In fact, most ancient cultures around the world seem to have some understanding of their existence. In China they are known as 'dragon lines', in South America the shamans refer to them as 'spirit lines' and in Australia the first nation people call them 'dream lines'.

Ley lines are also said to be able to take information or energy from their higher vibrational points and carry it around the world, spreading knowledge and wisdom to all inhabitants.

For more information, on ley line research check out Alfred Watkins' *The Old Straight Track* (Watkins, 1988), John Michell's *The View Over Atlantis* (Michell, 2017) and the work of the Earth Mysteries Movement

Research into ley lines' locations is more advanced in some countries than others. In the UK and Europe it is reasonably easy to find a ley line near you, but in other countries that knowledge may not be so easy to come by. A Google search will no doubt give you pointers. There are those that suggest that spending too much time near a ley line is unwise, and living on one should probably be avoided, particularly if you are sensitive to subtle energy. However, visiting them, connecting and tapping into the energy in these locations can be beneficial because it allows us to connect with higher vibrational energy, or source energy. Where I live in the south of England, I am close to the line that runs from Eastbourne to Glastonbury. I often go to Cissbury Ring, an ancient landmark on the route, and thus connect with the energy of Glastonbury (or Avalon), 170 miles away.

6.1.5 Church sites

Although it may appear odd to connect the Earth's energy with the relatively modern religious structures that are associated with man's creation of religion, churches tended to be located on the sites of older pagan worshipping locations, and used some of the same techniques to locate them. The word 'pagan' is used here to describe the pre-Christian knowledge and culture intrinsic in the life of ancient peoples, which reflects their deeply understood connection with nature, spirit and existence itself. So, when visiting churches, remember that you are connecting with spiritual and divine sources, not religious icons. I've done this myself in Avebury, Glastonbury and other locations, and I've had some interesting experiences.

6.2 The Earth's seven chakra centres

The idea of chakras spans centuries, much further than does modern medicine. As discussed above, they relate to the seven places on the body from which energy is said to come: the root, sacral, solar plexus, heart, throat, third eye and crown. They're known first and foremost by their Sanskrit names, and it's said that they also relate to places around the globe that correspond to them, with unique energies that are far stronger than any other in the world (Machado, 2021). Visiting these places with humility, reverence and without expectation allows us the opportunity to connect more directly with source energy and be open to what needs to come to us at the time—and also whatever we need to give at that time. The seven sacred Earth chakra locations are as follows:

Root chakra: Mount Shasta, California

Muladhara, the root chakra, is located in the base of the spine; this is the point that roots us to the Earth and ourselves. Mount Shasta has been said to embody this process of grounding. It was long believed by first nation American peoples that this dormant volcano had healing powers and a spiritual nature about it that many people can feel when they're near.

Sacral chakra: Lake Titicaca, Peru/Bolivia

This lake borders is said to be Svadhishthana, the earth chakra. It is the highest navigable lake in the world and the largest in South America. It's believed that it has a place in mythology and may have even been the birthplace of mythological royalty (Summers, 2020). The lake itself is said to emit qualities that are both feminine and masculine, and to be the core for creativity and self-expression, as the sacral chakra is in the human body.

Solar plexus: Uluru, Australia

The Earth's Manipura, or solar plexus chakra, is a sandstone rock formation that is sacred to Australia's first nation peoples. It is a World Heritage Site, which is part of the reason why it attracts so many visitors year after year, but there may be more to it than that. Uluru is said to have great energy that can be re-energising and help a person reach their higher self, and it's possible that those who visit have picked up on this, as well. The history of Uluru is carved into its rock face and with 600 million years behind it, it's easy to believe there's sacred power in this area of Australia.

Heart: Stonehenge, Glastonbury and Shaftesbury, UK

Anahata is the heart chakra and Stonehenge, Glastonbury and Shaftesbury are believed to be its correspondents on Earth. Stonehenge is said to correspond with forgiveness and giving, two traits that Anahata is responsible for.

Throat: Mount of Olives, the Sphinx and Great Pyramids, Israel/Egypt

The Great Pyramid was built with lunar and solar alignments in mind, and is also said to be the place of the Vishuddha chakra. The celestial alignment of each design in ancient Egypt corresponds to the harmony that exists in one's thoughts, mind and speech. The chakra is responsible for the gift of speaking one's truth, and this region of Egypt is believed to enhance and embody that, as well.

Third Eye: Different locations, depending on the aeon

The third eye chakra, known as Ajna, is interesting because there is no fixed site for it. During our aeon—a time period with a cycle of 2,160 years—it is said to be in Stonehenge. This will change in a few centuries, and this chakra may move to another chakra's geolocation.

Crown: Mount Kailas, Himalayas

Also known as the 'stairway to heaven' and the crown chakra, Sahasrara can be found on Mount Kailas. The Himalayas have long been believed to hold their own powers and, for some, it's not just a result of their humbling nature as they tower over the rest of the Earth. This chakra is associated with knowledge and wisdom, as well as universal consciousness, so it's perfectly fitting that it would be located in this area.

6.3 Sacred sites by continent

Africa

Egypt

- Giza Plateau, the Great Pyramid, Sphynx and many other pyramids and structures whose real purpose is not fully understood. Aligned with the Orion constellation, as seen from Earth 12,000 years ago.

South America

Bolivia

- Puma Punku, Tiwanacu—high-tech megaliths.

Peru

- Sacsayhuaman, Cusco, Ollantaytambo—ancient high-tech megaliths
- Machu Picchu—magnificent mountain citadel
- Caral Supe, North of Limax—site of ancient pyramid and city, aligned with the Pleiades as seen from Earth. This is dated at 4,600 BP at least, predating the Incas by over 2,000 years and challenging the established chronology of human development on Earth
- Nazca Lines—ancient desert geoglyphs in the Nazca Desert.

Chile

- Easter Island—1,000 ancient carved monumental statues, or moai. The method of construction is still debated.

Asia

Japan

- Mount Kurama, Tokyo—where Mikao Usui received reiki symbols through meditation in the early twentieth century
- Yonaguni Jima, Ryukyu Islands, Okinawa—ancient underwater city, including megalithic structures and pyramids.

Micronesia

- Nan Madol, Temwen Island, Pohnpei—Ancient megalithic structures in a technically complex city.

Tibet, Himalayas

- Mount Kailash—ancient sacred site, thought of as the Crown Chakra of Planet Earth. Considered sacred in many religions, including Hinduism and Buddhism. The shape of the mountain is considered by some to replicate a pyramid.

Cambodia

- Angkor Wat—Largest religious site on Earth, possibly built 2600 BP. Believed to have multiple otherworldly features

Europe

UK

- Glastonbury Tor, Somerset
- Stonehenge, Wiltshire
- Avebury, Wiltshire
- West Kennet Barrow, Wiltshire
- Cissbury Ring, Findon Valley, Sussex
- Kingley Vale, Sussex
- Orkey Islands—Neolithic Orkney World Heritage Site, 'Ness of Brodgar'
- South Downs, Sussex, Kent, Hampshire.

Ireland

- New Grange Passage Tomb in Donore, Co Meath

France

- Carnac, Brittany—ancient megalithic site

Malta

- Megalithic temples, the Hypogeum of Hal Saflieni, and unexplained megalithic structures and underground complexes

Turkey

- Göbekli Tepe, near the present-day city of Şanlıurfa, is a neolithic archaeological site.

North America

USA

- Sedona, Arizona (Vortex)

The ancient Yavapai people lived in this area, painting petroglyphs and establishing cliff dwellings, indicating to future archaeologists and visitors that their creative force, the energy of their 'Great Mother' was powerful and palpable.

- Mount Shasta, California (Earth Root Chakra)
- Serpent Mound, Near Peebles, Ohio—An ancient serpent-shaped earth mound. There is a debate over its date of creation and purpose, but it may be more than 2,000 years old. The Serpent concept appears throughout the historical record and lore of many ancient cultures, including the Old Testament concept of Adam and Eve and the garden of Eden. Some have likened the pictorial depiction of the serpent to the human DNA strand, suggesting that it represents knowledge.

Australia

Uluru, Northern Territory

- Mystical, ancient rock with 348m above ground and 2.5km underground, considered to be the solar plexus chakra of Planet Earth. Of extreme significance to indigenous peoples, considered to be sacred and alive with history. Uluru, along with Kata Tjuta nearby, are considered to be living, breathing cultural landscapes.

Brisbane Water National Park, New South Wales

- Ancient Aboriginal rock art and carvings, considered to be between 8,000 and 10,000 years old, includes depictions of creator being (sky-hero from the Milky Way). Also includes the Gosford Glyphs, ancient carvings depicting Egyptian hieroglyphs that tell the story of a historic event that took place around 4,600 BP. See, for example, W Raymond Johnson, director of the Epigraphic Survey, and episode seven of *Ancient Aliens*, season eleven (Aliens, 2009).

Antarctica

Koettlitz glacier in Scott Coast

- Pyramid structure

Bibliography

Ancient Aliens (2009). Retrieved from Prometheus Entertainment: www.prometheusentertainment.com.
Avner, JR (September 2006). 'Altered States of Consciousness'. Pediatrics in Review, pp331-338.
Bakken, EE (2016). *Taking Charge of your Health and Well Being: Therapeutic Touch*. University of Minnesota.
Bauval, R (1989). Discussions in Egyptology, volume 13.
Beck, G (1993). *Sonic Theology: Hinduism and Sacred Sound*. University of South Carolina Press.
Bloomfield, M (1899). *The Arthavaveda*. Harvard University Press: Cambridge, Massachusetts.
Bohm, DJ (1980). *Wholeness and the Implicate Order*. Routledge: London.
Brace, P (2020). *Altered States of Consciousness: Natural Gateway to an Ecological Civilization?* Journal of Theoretical and Philosophical Psychology, 40(2), pp69–84.
Brink, NE (2016). *Trance Journeys of the Hunter Gatherers: Ecstatic Practices to Reconnect with the Great Mother and Heal the Earth*. Bear & Co: Rochester, Vermont.
British Medical Association (2019). Get a Move On: Steps to Increase Physical Activity Levels in the UK. British Medical Association.

Byrne, R (2006). *The Secret.* Simon & Schuster: London.

Canfield, J, Hansen MV, Newmark, A (2013). *Chicken Soup for the Soul, 20th Anniversary Edition.* Retrieved from www.chickensoup.com.

Canfield, J, Switzer, J (2005). *The Success Principles: How to Get from Where You Are to Where You Want to Be.* Chicken Soup for the Soul Publishing: New York.

Cronkleton, E, Wilson, DR (2019). *Aromatherapy: Uses and Benefits.* Retrieved from Healthline.

Cuts, C (2022). *Reiki Crystals.* Retrieved from Cosmic Cuts

De Stefano, M (2021). *Initiation,* Gaia.

Einstein, A (1936). Letter of 24 January 1936 to a Schoolgirl, Phyllis Wright.

Emoto, M (2004). *The Hidden Messages in Water.* Pocket Books.

Gaia (2017). *What Does Gaia Mean?* Retrieved from Gaia: https://www.gaia.com/article/meaning-of-gaia

Garcia, H, Miralles, F (2016). *Ikigai: The Japanese Secret to a Long and Happy Life.* Hutchinson: London.

Gattefosse, RM (1937). *Gattefosse's Arometherapy.* CW Daniel.

Gilbert, P (2009). *The Compassionate Mind.* Robinson: London.

Hancock, G. (2019). *America Before, The Key to Earth's Lost Civilisation.* St Martins Publishing Group: New York.

Harrison, E (1993). *Teach Yourself to Meditate: Over 20 Simple Exercises for Peace, Health and Clarity of Mind.* Judy Piatkus: London

Headspace. (2021). *What is Meditation?* Retrieved from headspace.com.

Hill, N (1937). *Think and Grow Rich.* Meriden, The Ralston Society: Connecticut.

Kanaga (2016). *Ley Lines: Earsth's Energy Grid* (Kanaga Series 8th Episode). Retrieved from Kanaga TV

Kent, KW (2017). *GodSpace: Embracing the Inconvenient Adventure of Intimacy with God*. Faithwords.

Kenyon, T, Sion, J (2002). *The Magdalen Manuscript: The Alchemies of Horus & The Sex Magic of Isis*. ORB Communications.

Larsen, S, Verner, T (2017). *The Transformational POWER of DREAMING, Discovering the Wishes of the Soul*. Inner Traditions: Rochester, Vermont.

Le Cunff, AL (2022). *Altered States of Consciousness: the Elusiveness of the Mind*. Retrieved from Ness Labs.

Lin, Y, (2021). *11 Essential Oils: Their Benefits and How to Use Them*. Retrieved from Cleveland Clinic, Health Essentials.

Long, B (1995). *Meditation, A Foundation Course. A Book of Ten Lessons*. Barry Long Books: London.

Machado, K. (2021). 'Earth Chakras: These Seven Locations around the World Are Believed to be Sacred'. Retrieved from TheTravel.com.

Mazzola, M and Greer, S (Directors) (2020). *Close Encounters of the Fifth Kind* [Motion Picture].

McCoy, E (1999). *Astral Projection for Beginners*. LLewellyn Publications: Woodbury, MN.

Metzner, R (2006). *The Ayahuasca Experience: A Sourcebook on the Sacred Vine of Spirits*. Park Street Press: Toronto.

Michaels, M, Johnson, P (2006). *The Essence of Tantric Sexuality*. Llewellyn Publications: Rochester, Vermont.

Michell, J (2017). *View over Atlantis*. Discover Books: Toledo.

Neff, K, Germer, C (2018). *The Mindful Self-Compassion Workbook: A Proven Way to Accept Yourself, Build Inner Strength and Thrive*. The Guildford Press: New York.

Nelson, AD (2016). *Origins of Consciousness: How the Search to Understand the Nature of Consciousness is Leading to a New View of Reality*. Lulu.com.
Nelson, R (2009). *What is the Nature of Global Consciousness?* Retrieved from The Global Consciousness Project.
Nolan, C (Director) (2010). *Inception* [Motion Picture].
Nunez, K, Fontane, D (2020). *What are Flower Essences?* Retrieved from Healthline.
Parker, KL, Lambert, J (1993). *Wise Women of the Dreamtime: Aboriginal Tales of the Ancestral Powers*. Inner Traditions International: Rochester, Vermont.
Pathfinder Ewing (Nvnehi Awatsigi), J (2011). *Dreams of the Reiki Shaman*. Findhorn Press: Rochester, Vermont.
Patton, L (2004). *Veda and Upanishad in the Hindu World*. Routledge: Abingdon, UK.
Ra, K (2016). *The Sophia Code: a Living Transmission from the Sophia Dragon Tribe*. Kaia Ra & Ra-El Publishing: Mount Shasta, California.
Robbins, A (1989). *Unlimited Power: The New Science of Personal Achievement*. Simon & Schuster: London.
Safron, A (2016, Vol 6, Issue 1). 'What is Orgasm? A Model of Sexual Trance and Climax via Rhythmic Entrainment'. Socioaffective Neuroscience and Psychology.
Sayin, HÜ (2015, V1, Iss 1). 'Altered States of Consciousness Occurring during Expanded Sexual Response (ESR) in the Human Female: Preliminary Definitions'. SexuS Journal, pp1-90.
Schlemmer, PV, Jenkins, P (1993). *The Only Planet of Choice, Essential Briefings from Deep Space*. Gateway Books: Bath.
Sophrology Academy (2021). Homepage. Retrieved from SophrologyAcademy.
Storr, A (1998). *The Essential Jung, Selected Writings, Intro-*

duced by Anthony Storr. Fontana: London.
Summers, C (2020). *Exploring the Earth Chakras: Sacred Sites and Ancient Wisdom*. Retrieved from www.artisanfarmacy.com.
Thakar, VJ (2010, December). 'Historical Development of Basic Concepts of Ayurveda from Veda up to Samhita'. AYU: An International Quarterly Journal of Research in Ayurveda, pp400-402.
Vazhakunnathu, T (2020). *Spiritual Theory of Everything*. Amazon: UK.
Von Däniken, E (1968). *Chariot of the Gods? Unsolved Mysteries of the Past*. Putnam: USA.
Wachowski, L (Director) (1999). *The Matrix* [Motion Picture].
Watkins, A (1988). *The Old Straight Track: Its Mounds, Beacons, Moats, Sites and Mark Stones*. Abacus.
Wattles, WD (1910). *The Science of Getting Rich*. Elizabeth Towne Compant: Holyoke, Massachusetts.
Wittmann, M (2018). *Altered States of Consciousness: Experiences Out of Time and Self*. The MIT Press: London.
Witzel, M (2003). "Vedas and Upanisads", in *The Blackwell Companion to Hinduism*. Blackwell: Oxford.
Yogananda, P (1946). *Autobiography of a Yogi*. The Philosophical Library: New York.
— (1925). *The Science of Religion*. Self Realization Fellowship

Index

Your story—ready to inspire others?

If you would like to share your story and help and inspire others to explore their practical spirituality, then please get in touch on sharemystory@consciousnessawaken.org. There is a template that can be shared to help you frame your story, or you can find your flow and just let your stream of consciousness loose on your keyboard.

Namaste

About the author

Anthony Oyo is a seeker. Since his own "paradigm shifting" spiritual awakening over thrity years ago, he has explored the meaning of existence, the nature and purpose of humanity and individuality. He has developed his own meditation practice and trained to give back as a reiki master teacher and practitioner, and practical spirituality life coach. In parallel, he has worked towards embracing the responsibilities, challenges and opportunities of family life and corporate roles in the engineering and international development spheres, which he has carried out all over the world. As a qualified mediator, Anthony has also been active in developing the idea of compassion-based mediation, primarily for use in violent conflict prevention and resolution.

In line with his purpose to raise the vibration of human consciousness, he has been guided to create this book, along with some extraordinary contributors. The aim is to provide practical guidance for those seeking some "how to" steps to try out themselves and make movements towards achieving their own practical spirituality aspirations, in balance with their everyday lives.

This book is not about escape. Of course, if you have the desire and means to acquire and set up residence in your

Himalayan cave, where you will dwell and meditate for the rest of this human experience, then fantastic—please take a copy of this book to read in the in-between times. But for the rest of us, who consciously do not want to escape to the cave, and are happy to continue with the challenges and opportunities of living an Earthbound life (families, money, mortgages, jobs, houses, etc, etc), then this book draws on twelve approaches to support the development of your spiritual practice and to attempt to achieve some balance. These tools are a reflection of the authors own life experience, over thirty years since his own awakening. These are supported by twelve amazing real-life stories from friends and family who were brave and courageous enough to sit down and write their own journeys with practical spirituality, to hopefully provide some wisdom and inspiration for others.

You can find out more through www.consciousnessawaken.org.